DATE	ISSUED TO
AP 2 8 '89	504
FE 4 '92	1836
OC 17 '07	

Christmas Trees
for Pleasure and Profit

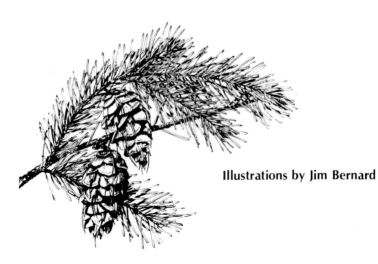

Illustrations by Jim Bernard

Christmas Trees
for Pleasure and Profit

Arthur G. Chapman
Robert D. Wray

Third Edition

Rutgers University Press
New Brunswick, New Jersey

Third Edition, Second Printing, 1987

Library of Congress Cataloging in Publication Data

Chapman, Arthur Glenn, 1895 –
 Christmas trees for pleasure and profit.

 Bibliography: p.
 Includes index.
 1. Christmas trees. I. Wray, Robert D.
II. Title.
SB428.C46 1985 634.9'75 84-15025
ISBN 0-8135-1074-0

CONTENTS

PREFACE TO THIRD EDITION

Several important changes have taken place in the Christmas tree industry since 1979 when our original book was revised and the second edition published. The use of herbicides to prepare planting sites and control weeds in established plantations has burgeoned as new, safer, more selective chemicals have been developed and registered for use. Species preferences have shifted to the extent that Scotch pine now shares its dominance of the market with Douglas-fir and other short-needled varieties. And new types of machines—trimmers, sprayers, cutters—continue to make the work easier and faster.

This third edition incorporates these changes and dwells at some length on the one having the greatest impact—herbicide use. But, again, the fundamentals of growing Christmas trees do not change much with time, even though the mechanics do. So, this new edition, while acknowledging the changing processes, continues to stress the basic principles.

Once more, help was generously given and gratefully received in this effort. The following warrant special mention: Dr. John F. Ahrens, Connecticut Agricultural Experiment Station, for providing advice on and information for the sections dealing with herbicides. Dr. Thomas H. Nicholls, North Central Forest Experiment Station, Forest Service, U.S. Department of Agriculture, for offering advice and providing photographs. Dr. Darroll D. Skilling, North Central Forest Experiment Station, Forest Service, U.S. Department of Agriculture, for carefully reviewing the previous edition, recommending revisions, and providing photographs.

PREFACE

This is a revised and slightly expanded version of the first edition of our book, *Christmas Trees for Pleasure and Profit,* published in 1957. Twenty years ago growing Christmas trees was still a relatively new idea. To be sure, Christmas tree farms were becoming more and more a part of the landscape, especially in the northeastern and Great Lakes states. But plantation-grown trees were just beginning to make themselves known in the market. During the past two decades, however, the business has grown and many refinements have been made. Better tools and faster methods for shearing have been devised; the use of chemical poisons (pesticides) to control weeds, insects, and diseases has been all but revolutionized; the use of artificial colorants has become common practice; and the industry has become more mechanized. Despite these new developments, however, the principles governing the growing of trees have remained the same—only the practices have changed. So, although we discuss and illustrate practices throughout the book, we put most emphasis on basic principles, knowing that specific tools and techniques will vary with time and place.

As is always the case with a work such as this, many others contributed in various ways to the revision. Grateful thanks are extended to

Marvin E. Smith, extension forester, University of Minnesota, for reviewing the original book and suggesting where changes were needed, and for providing photographs.

Louis F. Wilson, research entomologist, North Central

Forest Experiment Station, U.S. Forest Service, for providing updated information and new photographs for the section on insects.

Thomas H. Nicholls and Darroll D. Skilling, research pathologists, North Central Forest Experiment Station, U.S. Forest Service, for helping to revise and illustrate the section on diseases.

William H. Carmean, soil scientist, North Central Forest Experiment Station, U.S. Forest Service, for giving advice and suggestions on the discussions of pesticides.

J. R. Dilworth, professor, Department of Forest Science, Oregon State University, for providing information on the Christmas-tree industry in the Northwest.

Gary H. Sander, extension forestry specialist, Oregon State University, for providing photographs of Christmas-tree growing in the Northwest.

The following persons and organizations for providing photographs:

Philip H. Jones

Harry A. Lowther Company

Michigan State University

National Christmas Tree Association

Ohio Forestry Association

Gloria L. Wray, for so carefully typing and proofreading the manuscript revisions.

And finally, I want to make special mention of my longtime friend, colleague, and coauthor, Arthur G. Chapman. For reasons of health, "Chappie" was unable to contribute materially to this new version, and he passed away before it was published. But it is really *his* book. It was at his invitation that I joined him in this endeavor back in 1955. His knowledge and experience as a forester, scientist, research administrator, and Christmas-tree grower formed the backbone for the original book. That so much of what was said then is as true now as it was twenty years ago is a tribute to his wisdom and insight.

Robert D. Wray

1

A "GROWING" BUSINESS

This is a book about growing and selling Christmas trees. It is written for people who like to grow things, either as a hobby or as a business—for pleasure or for profit, or both. More specifically, it is for the farmer who has a few acres of land not suitable for ordinary crops and who would like to try something different; it is for the prospective commercial grower who might devote several hundred acres to Christmas trees. It is for the person who is seeking a hobby that will keep him outdoors and perhaps supplement his income, and for the person who would like to earn his entire living growing Christmas trees. It is for the person at or near retirement age who would like to keep busy and productive in his later years, but who does not want to be tied down by a regular routine. It is for the young person who would like a sideline business of his own that he could build up in his spare time through the years into a thriving enterprise. And in addition, it is for schools, youth organizations, sportsmen's clubs, and other civic and private groups that for various reasons would like to plant and maintain small "forests." In short, it is for anyone—regardless of means or motives—to whom the idea of growing Christmas trees sounds appealing.

Growing trees specifically for the Christmas-tree market is not a new or fly-by-night idea. Christmas-tree plantations were beginning to dot the countryside in some states nearly fifty years ago. At that time, most of the trees sold in this country were naturally grown, cut from wild land. But in the last twenty-five years the share of the live-tree market held by plantation-grown trees has expanded from 5 percent to more than 80 percent. And this trend will inevitably continue because cultivated trees are consistently better and more uniform in quality than wild trees. Moreover, wild trees are getting scarcer.

PLANTED VS. WILD TREES

The Christmas-tree supplier who cuts his trees from wild land must go where they are and bring them back to the consumer. As the sources for forest-grown trees become more and more remote, the quality of the trees is bound to suffer. The supplier is forced to cut and transport all the trees he can find instead of selecting only the better ones. He usually contracts for all the trees on a certain area and so feels obliged to take them all. This results in an increasing number of spindly, misshapen trees on the market.

Moreover, most forest-grown trees, especially in the East, are spruce and fir, species that dry out and lose their needles faster than the pines. So, after being cut, bundled, shipped long distances, handled, and stored since early fall, the wild trees that finally are set up and trimmed at Christmas in homes all over the country are likely to have dry, brittle, discolored needles that begin to fall off before the last ornament is hung. Such dried-out trees are a potential fire hazard, whereas fresh, green trees have been shown to be remarkably resistant to fire.

Planted trees, on the other hand, are properly spaced, cared for, and sheared to assure full foliage and symmetrical shape (*Fig. 1*). They are destined for the Christmas-tree market before they are even planted, and so everything done to them between planting and harvesting is calculated to fit them better for their intended use. Moreover, they are produced near enough to the market that they need not be cut until needed and can be delivered fresh and undamaged to the retailer.

Figure 1. Well-formed Scotch pines, one of the species most in demand for Christmas trees, ready for harvest.

Each year the supplier of wild trees has to go farther and look harder to find acceptable ones. But the plantation owner does not have to search for his trees; they have been right at hand for several years. He has been watching them grow and develop since they were seedlings, so he knows how many and what kind he will have ready for the market. He can invite a prospective wholesale buyer to come and view his product before closing a deal. In contrast, the wholesaler usually must buy forest-grown trees sight unseen.

Another factor favoring planted trees has been the changing taste for species. Years ago, spruce, fir, and redcedar were the standard species used. Then a desire for longer-needled, bushier-looking trees saw the pines dominating the market. Most pines currently on the market are grown in plantations. In fact, the most popular of the pines, Scotch pine, does not occur naturally in the Western Hemisphere, so the demand *must* be met by the plantation owner. A more recent trend, however, shows plantation-grown firs regaining favor and sharing more of the limelight with the pines.

NATURAL VS. ARTIFICIAL TREES

But what about artificial trees—those made of glittering aluminum and the almost-real-looking plastic ones? It is obvious that such trees have made large inroads into the market in recent years. In fact, in the early 1970s more than one-third of the Christmas trees purchased were artificial. To be sure, the convenience of an artificial tree has been a big selling point: you don't have to buy a new tree each year and you don't have to dispose of a used one. (You *do* have to assemble your plastic tree each year, of course, and then take it apart again and store it.) And you do get uniform quality—the "perfect" tree. But there are those who believe that demand for man-made trees will soon level off, if it has not already done so. Their reasoning is that the boom in artificial trees was partly the result of some mistaken notions about live trees.

One of these notions was that bringing a natural evergreen tree into your house posed a serious fire hazard. But the Christmas-tree industry responded by convincingly demonstrating that if a tree is fresh and green and kept in water, it is difficult to make it burn, even deliberately.

Another flurry of concern centered around the idea that cutting live trees was wasteful of an important natural resource and harmful to the environment. But here again, as people have become more knowledgeable about environmental matters, they have come to realize that Christmas-tree plantations enhance the landscape rather than harm it. In addition to making otherwise marginal land economically productive, plantations help control runoff and erosion, provide cover for wildlife, and beautify the countryside (*Fig. 2*).

The growing concern over energy conservation also favors the natural tree. The energy source for growing live

Figure 2. Christmas-tree plantations have aesthetic as well as economic value. (*U. S. Forest Service*)

trees—the sun—is limitless and free, but both aluminum and plastic products require excessive amounts of man-made energy in their manufacture. And further, the materials themselves—aluminum and petrochemicals—are limited in supply. When they are gone, there is no more. Trees, however, are a renewable resource; where you have harvested one you can grow another. To be sure, artificial trees will be around for a while, perhaps for a long time, but real ones will be around forever.

THE CURRENT OUTLOOK

Interest in growing Christmas trees has been increasing steadily during the past few years. Hundreds of new plantations are started every year. Some of them are successful and their owners enjoy a profitable, satisfying venture. Unfortunately, many fail because their owners have gone into the project blindly, not knowing what to do or how to do it.

Growing Christmas trees is a science and a business and must be treated as both. The grower must know how to select, plant, protect, maintain, and harvest his trees. That is science. And he must know when, where, and how to sell the trees he produces in order to make a profit on them. That is business.

Both the scientific and the business phases of growing trees will be discussed in this book. In actual practice they are inseparable. You cannot grow trees without considering costs and returns. And you cannot sell them if you do not know how to grow them.

The prospective grower will want to consider the Christmas-tree industry as a whole as it is today. And, what is more important, he will want to know something about the outlook for the business in five, ten, or twenty years. For if he were to plant a thousand seedlings now, it would be at least six years before any of them would be ready for the market.

Producing and selling Christmas trees is a multimillion-dollar business. About thirty million trees are sent to market each year in the United States alone. About 5 percent of these are imported from Canada; the rest are produced in the United States, chiefly in the northern states. Canada's contribution is mostly spruces, balsam fir, and Douglas-fir, although an increasing number of Scotch pine from plantations in the eastern provinces is reaching our markets.

Three species dominate the market for plantation-grown Christmas trees in the United States: Scotch pine, Douglas-fir, and balsam fir. Scotch pine had been the acknowledged leader until recently when the firs began gaining in popularity. The Northwest produces the bulk of the Douglas-fir while the Midwest and Northeast regions of the country supply most of the Scotch pine and balsam fir. Other pines (notably red and white), Norway and white spruce, and several firs plus some cedar make up the rest of the market.

What about the future? Is it likely that people will stop buying natural Christmas trees? Hardly. Despite the current popularity of artificial trees, the more than twelve thousand growers in the country usually have no trouble selling all the trees they can produce on their nearly half a million acres of plantations. For many people, the enjoyment of the fresh look and smell of a real tree in their living room still outweighs the convenience of a metal or plastic one.

One other trend should serve to encourage the Christmas-tree grower. The public is becoming more discriminating in its selection of Christmas trees. People are no longer satisfied with thin, scrawny, lopsided trees. Their taste no doubt has been influenced by the introduction in recent years of fresher, fuller, and more symmetrical plantation-grown trees.

Growing Christmas trees as a hobby or a business has several appealing features to recommend it aside from the fact that you may make some money at it. In the first place, most of the necessary work is done in spring, summer, and fall, when the working conditions are pleasant. During the winter the trees are fairly safe from fire, insects, disease, and weeds, and hence need little care (Fig. 3). After the harvest the grower can hibernate if he wants to, or go to Florida, until planting time in the spring.

Another advantage is that the beginner can start out on any scale, from one acre to a thousand, and make a capital investment accordingly. He can be a Christmas-tree grower by merely leasing an acre or two of land, buying a couple of thousand trees, and using the garden tools that he probably already has. The initial investment, then, need not run to more than two hundred dollars. On the other hand, if he wants to go into the business on a commercial scale, he can invest several thousand dollars in land, machinery, and labor.

Some of the work is strenuous, especially if done only with hand tools, but it need not be killing. And if the grower learns to use the tools skillfully and trains himself to take it easy, the work can be more pleasant than painful. In fact,

A "Growing" Business

Figure 3. Christmas trees demand little or no care during winter.
(*National Christmas Tree Association*)

most growers go in for Christmas trees primarily because they like the work. It is that kind of business.

Does all this sound good to you? If so, you may be tempted to run out and buy a few thousand seedlings, plant them indiscriminantly in the nearest patch of ground, and then sit back and wait for the profits to roll in. Some would-be growers have done just that in the past—with unfortunate results. There are many things to be considered and done before a tree can even be put into the ground. And what is done during the several years between the time the trees are planted and the time they are harvested will either make or break the venture.

2

SELECTING LAND

First comes the question of land. If you already have a patch of ground that is suitable for growing Christmas trees—an out-of-the-way corner of a farm perhaps—land is no problem. But if you are starting from scratch and have to look around for a planting site to buy or lease, three things must be considered: how much land, what kind, and where. Naturally, the final choice will be greatly influenced by what land is available in the locality and how much money can be invested.

HOW MUCH?

How much land you need depends upon you. If you just like to putter around with plants and would like a profitable hobby, two or three acres will probably be enough, especially if you expect to do all the work yourself by hand in your spare time. But if you plan to earn your living entirely from your Christmas-tree farm, a couple hundred acres or more will be needed. Some of the larger commercial farms occupy many hundreds of acres and employ dozens of workers. Huge plantations are the exception rather than the rule, however. The average Christmas-tree farm in many of the eastern states is about fifteen acres.

A natural question at this point is: how much land can one person manage by himself? Roughly speaking, if a man gets outside help for planting and harvesting, he can do all the rest of the work by himself on up to twenty acres. But this figure must not be taken too literally; it can change drastically up or down, depending upon topography, soil, ground cover, equipment used, and time spent. So if you can locate as many as eighty acres of good land that is easy to work, do not be afraid to tackle it alone.

WHAT KIND?

The very best planting site would be a gently rolling, well-drained area with a moderate amount of ground cover, workable soil, and no brush (*Fig. 4*). But such land is

Figure 4. Grassy fields with little or no brush cover are ideal for the planting and survival of Christmas-tree seedlings. (*U. S. Forest Service*)

probably either not for sale or is too expensive. Sharply rolling to hilly land is well suited for growing Christmas trees, as is so-called worn-out farmland. Either kind can usually be bought or leased for much less than good farmland.

Soil fertility is not a factor here because fertility is rarely a limiting factor in growing Christmas trees. Most land capable of producing any kind of vegetation at all is good enough for growing Christmas trees. In fact, it would be best to shy away from land that is too fertile. High fertility means rapid growth, and Christmas trees should not grow too fast. A moderate, uniform growth rate produces the best trees.

Another thing to avoid is land that is low, wet, and poorly drained. Some species of Christmas trees, such as balsam fir and black spruce, do grow naturally on very wet sites, but they do not thrive under these conditions, they merely tolerate them. And since other trees will not, the fir and spruce usually have the bogs to themselves. Both species do better on the uplands, however, where the soil is well drained and aerated.

Dry, gravelly sites are equally undesirable. Water runs off or through this kind of soil so fast that there is seldom enough moisture to supply the trees. Moreover, such land is likely to be rocky and hence difficult to work, especially with machinery.

If you are planning to plant and mow by machine (and if your operation is large enough, you should certainly seriously consider the use of machinery), topography will limit your selection of planting sites. Land that is generally too steep to maneuver a farm tractor on should be avoided. However, small patches of steep land can be left unplanted or be planted by hand. Therefore a site that is otherwise suitable should not be rejected because 10 percent or less of it will not permit the efficient use of machinery.

The site requirements of the species to be grown will also help determine the kind of land to use. Like any other plant, each Christmas-tree species will do best under certain growing conditions. For many species, however, the requirements are broad and very similar; if land is suitable for one species, it is more than likely suitable for most of the others that are known to grow successfully in the vicinity. There are a few exceptions, so it would be wise to review carefully the site requirements for the various species given in Chapter 3 before finally deciding on any particular piece of land. Some give-and-take will be necessary between selecting land to suit the species and selecting species to suit the land that is available.

WHERE?

Finally, there is the question of location. Here again there are several things to consider. The first one is distance to markets. In growing trees to sell, it is an advantage to produce the trees as close as possible to the intended market. Short hauling distance means low transportation cost and more profit.

Since the greatest market potential is in the large centers of population, a Christmas-tree farm should generally be located within a hundred miles of one or more large cities. This is especially important if you plan to produce several thousand trees per year. However, if you do locate farther than this from a city and do not plan a large operation, you may be in a good position to capture the smaller markets in nearby towns where there is less competition.

Accessibility is another important consideration. The land should be located adjacent to or very near a good road. The road need not be a main highway, or even paved for that matter. In fact, a gravel road has certain advantages over one that is paved. Such a road is usually less traveled and hence less apt to invite theft or vandalism. The only requirement is that it be passable by truck in all kinds of weather. Of course, if you find a piece of land favorable for growing trees in all other respects, but some distance from a good road, you may want to give it serious consideration. After all, you cannot expect to get land that will meet all the ideal specifications. On such a site, however, it will be necessary to haul harvested trees by sled or wagon from the plantation to the roadside. And it is axiomatic that the less the trees are handled between stump and truck, the better it is for both the grower and the trees.

For Christmas-tree farms on which several thousand trees are planted and harvested each year, a well-planned system of all-weather roads within the plantation is a good investment The ideal would be a network of roads so laid out that no tree would be more than one hundred yards from a road (*Fig. 5*).

Another reason for easy accessibility both to and throughout the plantation is protection from fire and other

Figure 5. Roads criss-crossing a plantation provide access to all the trees and serve as firebreaks as well. (*U.S. Forest Service*)

hazards. In case of fire or sudden insect infestation, you want to be able to get to the critical spot fast with the necessary equipment. And finally, for a "choose-and-cut" operation (see chapter 17), your plantation must be accessible to your customers.

COST

The price of suitable land is of major importance. The land represents the basic and perhaps greatest single investment, an investment that has to be made first, before any other steps can be taken.

Unfortunately, little can be said in a concrete way about land values except that they have skyrocketed in the past few years. Prices asked and paid for land to be used for

13

growing Christmas trees vary greatly according to region, locality, accessibility, topography, soil, and so on. Except under unusual circumstances, growers entering the Christmas-tree market today can expect to pay from three hundred to one thousand dollars per acre for suitable land. The important thing to remember is that this land is for growing trees, not farm crops. There is no need to invest in the best agricultural land you can find. On the other hand, the success of the venture should not be endangered by saddling yourself with a piece of inadequate land just because it is cheap.

Land that is subject to residential or industrial development should also be avoided. Growing Christmas trees is a long-term project and if the land should suddenly increase greatly in value, you could no longer afford to hold it for producing trees. Then you would have to start all over again somewhere else.

You can get help in locating a suitable piece of land and judging its value from a reliable real estate dealer, the local county agent, or your district farm forester. At any rate, choose the site carefully and deliberately. This decision is probably the most important one you will make; for it is the land, not the trees, that is the most valuable resource.

As a summary, here is a checklist of questions to ask when considering any piece of land:

Area—How much land do I need? Is there room for expansion?

Soil—Is it workable, neither too light nor too heavy, neither too wet nor too dry?

Topography—Is it level enough to permit the use of machinery? (Assuming you plan to use machinery.)

Surface—Is it reasonably free from dense brush, tree stumps, rocks?

Location—Is it near a good, all-weather road? How far is it from the major markets?

Adaptability—Will it support the species I want to grow?

Cost—Can I afford it?

3

SPECIES TO GROW

The next question that confronts a prospective Christmas-tree grower is what species to plant. A great deal of the financial success of the enterprise depends upon selection of the right species. Any mistake made at this point will be felt increasingly throughout the life of the trees and will be very costly in time and money.

When selecting the species that are right for you, three things must be considered: climate, site, and markets.

CLIMATE

The climate will, of course, limit the species to be grown. Trees, like other plants, have definite requirements as to maximum and minimum temperatures, amount of rainfall, and length of growing season. To be sure, many species have been translocated from one region to another and grown successfully; but to try to import a species out of its range without some strong evidence that it can be grown in your locality is to invite trouble. It is better to choose species native to the region or those that already have been successfully introduced.

Some species have wider ranges than others. White, red, and jack pine, for example, can be grown readily in most of the northern half of the United States and in adjacent areas in Canada. The spruces and firs, on the other hand, must have a cooler climate and seldom grow naturally south of New England, the Great Lakes, and the Northwest (except at high elevations).

SITE

Site means the specific environment a plant is growing in. It has to do chiefly with soil, moisture, and topography. Each species has a set of optimum site conditions under which it will do best. Some species seem to survive and grow best on high ridgetops where the soil is thin but competition from other plants is at a minimum. Others do best on the lower slopes where the soil is richer, deeper, and moister. Some thrive on the north side of a hill where it is cool, moist, and shady. Some grow best on south-facing slopes where they get sunlight all day. Some will tolerate acid soils; others will not.

If you have twenty or more acres of land, you may have several different sites on it and you may want to select a different species for each site. In fact, growing more than one species is usually considered good business; the vagaries of markets, climate, insects, diseases, and the like sometimes make it inadvisable to put all your eggs in one basket.

SOIL

Christmas trees do not require rich soil for good survival and growth. So it is usually not necessary to worry about the lack of essential mineral elements; the soil available probably contains all the elements necessary for producing good Christmas trees. However, if you suspect that some important element is lacking, the easiest way to find out is to send a sample of the soil to your state agricultural college for analysis. But this is only necessary in extreme cases; most soils are able to produce *some* kind of Christmas tree.

Soil characteristics that *may* be critical are texture (the size of the soil particles) and reaction (acidity).

The texture of the soil may range from very fine to coarse. Fine soils are the clays, or heavy soils, composed almost entirely of very small particles. Coarse soils are the sandy or light soils and are made up of larger particles that do not cling together like the clays. These are the two extremes; there are many variations of the two and many combinations as well. The best soils are the loams that have a texture about half way between the clays and the sands, and combine the best attributes of both.

The major importance of texture is that it influences the amount of water and air that the soil can hold. A clay soil holds more water than a sandy soil because the minute clay particles tend to trap the water in the tiny spaces between them, whereas water can more readily seep downward through the larger spaces in the lighter soils. By the same token, clay soils contain less air because the pore spaces are occupied with water. Both water and air are necessary to the roots of the trees, but some plants need more water than others, hence the difference in soil requirements among species.

Soil reaction—whether it is acid or alkaline—is expressed in numerical terms called *pH*. A soil that is neutral has a pH of 7.0. Numbers higher than that indicate an alkaline soil; lower numbers indicate an acid soil. Soil reaction is critical only at extremes. Most coniferous trees, except for the cedars, grow naturally and well in slightly acid soils; a pH of 6.0 or higher is considered ideal. However, low, wet, poorly drained soils that tend to be excessively acid are to be avoided. This condition slows the bacterial action in the soil, which in turn interferes with the availability of nutrients to the trees. In rare instances, when other conditions are favorable, it may be worth trying to work with a strongly acid soil (pH less than 5.0) by neutralizing it with lime. But here again, it would be wise to seek the advice of local experts.

Fertilizing

One of the questions that confronts the beginning grower is whether to fertilize. Fertilizing to stimulate growth is rarely necessary because most Christmas trees, especially the pines, grow too fast anyway. In fact, in a well-managed plantation, part of each year's growth is cut off to give the trees a more dense, uniform appearance.

Normally, an evergreen tree develops a new set of lateral branches (called a *whorl*) each year. The distance between these whorls represents a year's height growth. If this distance is too great (eight inches or more), the tree develops an open, ragged-looking crown. Rapid growth then only increases the frequency and intensity of shearing that must be done. More about this later.

Some growers do fertilize their trees under certain circumstances and for specific purposes. One fairly common practice is to fertilize at the time of planting. This stimulates growth during that first critical year or two when trees are competing with other low vegetation for a place in the sun. Such a practice may be especially appropriate for the slower-growing species such as the spruces and firs.

Another specific use for fertilizer is to improve the vigor and color of the needles just before harvesting. Some Christmas trees, particularly the pines, tend to fade to a yellowish color in the fall, lowering their value on the market. One way to help prevent this, especially on light, sandy soils, is to fertilize some time during the final year of growth.

Whether, when, and how much to fertilize your trees will depend upon the conditions in your specific locality. The best way to find out is to talk with experienced growers in your area or to consult your county agent or extension forester. But the basic principle remains: don't do anything to your plantation—including fertilizing—that you aren't fairly sure will pay for itself in the long run.

MARKET

Climate and site determine to a large extent what species *can* be grown; the market will very often reveal what species *should* be grown. If you are growing Christmas trees to sell, you must grow species that the people in your locality will buy. The market demand for various Christmas-tree species may be quite different from region to region. The various tastes in species have been affected chiefly by two things: tradition and availability. And in recent years, preferences have changed radically, especially in certain localities.

In the past, certain kinds of evergreen trees were considered to be "Christmas trees" and no others would do. A good example is the traditional preference for spruce and fir in the northeastern states. This tradition grew mainly out of necessity; certain species were the only ones available in some areas for so long that to suggest any other seemed like bringing in an imposter. But in more recent years, this "evergreen curtain" has been broken down and several new species have successfully invaded some heretofore very limited markets.

The change has come partly by choice and partly by necessity. As the traditional species—the native spruces and firs—became scarcer in the wild, the pines began to catch the fancy of the people in some localities and soon dominated the market. But then plantation-grown spruces and firs showed up, recapturing some of the earlier popularity of their wild-grown cousins.

The upshot of all this: there are differences among markets and it will pay any potential Christmas-tree grower to find out what species move best in his locality. The way to do this is to visit the larger cities nearby between Thanksgiving and Christmas and see. Get acquainted with some of the retailers, tell them why you are interested, and spend some time in their lots observing the buyers.

The introduction of plantation-grown trees and new species has stimulated greater discrimination on the part of the typical Christmas-tree buyer. Although some customers still ask for "one of those bushy trees with the long needles,'' or ''a real dark green one,'' or ''one shaped like an ice-cream cone,'' many of them now know the species by name and are very discerning about such things as needle vigor, color, and retention. But whether the people in your area buy their trees by species or not, they still buy them according to shape, size of needles, and color. (All Christmas trees are green, of course, unless they are artificially colored, but they range in shade from light to dark green and in hue from yellow green to blue green.) So when you have satisfied yourself that you know *what* shape, *what* needle size, and *what* color are preferred, you can translate this information into corresponding species. Then you can decide which of several preferred species will grow best in your climate and on your site.

SPECIES

Following is a description of the major Christmas-tree species: what they look like, how they differ, their climate and site requirements, and how much sales appeal they have. Four different kinds are especially considered: the pines, the spruces, the firs, and others.

Pines

The most distinguishing feature of the pines is their long needles, rarely less than one and a half inches, which occur in small bundles or clusters, ranging from two to five needles per cluster, depending upon the species. As a group they are the fastest growing of the Christmas trees. Rarely used as Christmas trees in this country until the early 1950's, they grew steadily in popularity for the next thirty years.

Scotch pine. Scotch pine, the most popular of the pines, is a native of Europe. Introduced into the United States and Canada many years ago as a timber tree, it largely failed as such. It has, however, rapidly won increasing favor as a

Christmas tree, especially in the northeastern states, in the eastern provinces of Canada, and on the Pacific Coast. There are many varieties or strains of Scotch pine that differ a great deal in length, color, and stiffness of the needles, and in stem form. The best strains have needles one and a half to two inches long, an eye-catching blue green color, and rather flexible needles (*Fig. 1*). Less desirable strains are grass green in color and have long, stiff needles and coarse stems and branches. Even the best strains sometimes have crooked stems.

Although this tree grows well in a wide range of site conditions, the best sites are old fields with sandy loam soil of no more than moderate fertility. However, avoid altitudes of more than three or four thousand feet, poorly drained wet soils, and extremely dry ridges or upper slopes. As do most pines, Scotch pine grows rapidly, attaining Christmas-tree size in six or seven years. It responds well to shearing and retains its needles and color for four to six weeks after cutting.

The most objectionable feature of Scotch pine is that the foliage of some strains may turn yellow in late fall. This untimely phenomenon occurs more in the grass green strains than in the blue green. Research is constantly underway to develop strains resistant to this tendency.

Red pine. This species is native to the Lake states, New England, northern Pennsylvania, New York, Connecticut, West Virginia, and southeastern Canada. It is the preferred tree of many users and is especially popular in larger sizes for churches, schools, business offices, stores, and entertainment halls.

Red pine has long needles which, like Scotch pine needles, are retained well for four to six weeks after cutting. The color is dark green and usually persists through the harvest season unless the needles become infected with a needle cast that may give them a reddish brown tint. Although the desired characteristics are quite constant in the species, there are some minor variations in branching among trees from different sources.

Red pine is planted far beyond its natural range, as far south as the Middle Atlantic states and as far west as Missouri and Iowa. It is frequently killed in western Iowa and on the edge of the plains, however, during dry, cold winters. It survives and develops satisfactorily on moderately dry sites, but does best on well-drained, sandy, and clay loams with good moisture and average fertility. It should not be planted on extremely dry ridges or in swampy, poorly drained soils. The trees respond well to shearing, but cannot be shaped into the desired form as early as most other pines. Hence, seven or eight years are required for the average rotation (growing span).

White pine. The eastern white pine occurs naturally throughout southeastern Canada, the Lake states, New England, and the Appalachian highlands as far south as Georgia. It is a favorite of many customers, but is usually produced and sold locally because it is too bushy and brittle to be shipped long distances.

The needles are uniformly bluish green in color and range between two and a half and three and a half inches long. After cutting, the needles and needle color are retained until well past the holiday season.

Unfortunately, white pine may suffer severe damage from deer and rabbits. It is susceptible to air pollutants from power plants and, at the edge of the plains, to extreme, dry cold. It will grow well on most sites except swamps and very dry, infertile soils. The tree grows rapidly, attaining Christmas-tree size in six or seven years, and therefore requires shearing to give it the proper symmetry and crown density (*Fig. 6*).

Austrian pine. This is another immigrant from Europe. It is grown on a relatively small scale for Christmas trees in the northeastern and some of the middle western states. The demand for it, however, is rather limited. Austrian pine

Figure 6. An eastern white pine kept dense in foliage and good in form by shearing.

can grow on very poor soil, but, like other pines used for Christmas trees, it should not be planted on wet, poorly drained land. It is also subject to winter damage in the northern latitudes and to Dothistroma needle blight.

Generally, the characteristics of this species are not as desirable as those of the other pines described. The needles are dark green, somewhat longer than those of red pine, stiff and sharp pointed. The trees retain their needles very well in warm, dry rooms. Usually growth is rapid, which means that shearing is necessary to obtain good form. Branches of the Austrian pine are thick and stiff, a factor which makes handling difficult. It is, however, an excellent tree for flocking.

Other pines. Other pines sometimes planted for Christmas trees include jack pine and the southern pines, chiefly Virginia, pitch, shortleaf, loblolly, longleaf, and slash. In California work is under way to manage Monterey, Bishop, and Beach pines, all native, for Christmas trees. Furthermore, experiment stations are attempting to develop hybrid pines suitable for Christmas trees.

Spruces

The spruces have short needles, rarely more than an inch long, that occur singly and are stiff and pointed and nearly rectangular in cross section. These trees are slower growing than the pines, more symmetrical in shape, and therefore require less shearing. One of the traditional species used for Christmas trees, spruce is still very popular, especially in the northern part of the United States and Canada.

Norway spruce. Imported from Europe many years ago, Norway spruce is commonly planted in the northeastern United States and eastern Canada for timber, landscaping, and Christmas trees. Most of the characteristics of the species are highly desirable for Christmas trees. Its needles are dark green and from one-half to one inch long. The tree has good form naturally and requires little shearing (*Fig. 7*).

Figure 7. Norway spruce, an immigrant from Europe, is popular in the Northeast. (*U. S. Forest Service*)

Its only serious weakness is its poor needle retention.

Norway spruce is well suited to a cool, moist climate and develops best on protected north or east slopes that have moist, well-drained soil. This species should not be planted on dry ridges or slopes where soils are thin and low in fertility. Growth rate varies greatly from place to place and so it may take anywhere from eight to fifteen years to produce trees of salable size.

White spruce. The natural range of white spruce extends from Newfoundland and Labrador westward across Canada to British Columbia and Alaska. In the United States it is found locally in Montana, Wyoming, the Black Hills, northern Minnesota, Wisconsin, Michigan, northern New York, and New England. It has been grown successfully for Christmas trees far beyond its range, from the Middle Atlantic states west to Missouri and Iowa.

Except for the fact that it loses its needles rather quickly in warm rooms, white spruce has all the desired features of a good Christmas tree. Its branches are slender and its blue green foliage dense (*Fig. 8*). Needles are short, varying from about one-half to one inch in length. When crushed, they emit a pungent odor that may be avoided if trees are handled carefully.

Planting should be confined to the cooler northern states or higher altitudes farther south. Soils of average fertility with good moisture are best. If possible, this species should be planted on protected slopes but will do quite well on undulating or gently rolling land if the soil is favorable. It grows more slowly than Norway spruce, usually requiring ten to fifteen years to produce a crop. It seldom requires much shearing.

Red spruce. This species grows naturally from Prince Edward Island and the St. Lawrence valley to northern Pennsylvania, in the New England states, and south in the Allegheny highlands to North Carolina and Tennessee. General form and qualities are good; but like all spruce

Figure 8. A premium grade white spruce. (*University of Minnesota, Agricultural Extension Service*)

species, red spruce loses its needles rapidly in warm rooms. Needles are dark green in color and about one-half inch in length. This species is planted mainly in the northeastern states.

Red spruce is planted rather sparingly for Christmas trees (although it serves this purpose well), chiefly because it usually takes twelve to twenty years to reach salable size. Planting should be done on well-drained soils in protected sites.

Other spruces. Colorado blue, Black Hills, black, and Engelmann spruce are all used to some extent as Christmas trees. Only the Colorado blue and the Black Hills spruce are known to be planted for the purpose. Both are slow growing. Of the two, the blue spruce has more attractive foliage and holds its needles better. Otherwise their qualities closely resemble those of the other spruces described above.

Douglas-fir. Botanically, this is not a true fir; it is one of the spruces. But it closely resembles the firs in appearance and growth characteristics. Only the Rocky Mountain form is considered here. Its natural range is the Rocky Mountains from southern British Columbia and Alberta to northern Mexico. Some Christmas trees of this species come from wild land, but trees from plantations are increasing in popularity in the northeastern states as well as in the West.

Douglas-fir has all the good qualities of an ideal Christmas tree. Needles are three-fourths to one and one-fourth inches long and vary by strains from yellow green to gray green and blue green (*Fig. 9*). Needle retention is good in warm rooms. Response to shearing is good, resulting in a more symmetrical tree with denser foliage than most of the wild land trees.

It is a slow grower, requiring up to ten years or more to develop into desired size. Trees grow best on moist, well-drained sites; tight clays and dry ridges and slopes should be avoided. It is by far the most-favored Christmas-tree

Figure 9. Douglas-fir, another very popular species, especially in the West.

species in the Pacific Northwest, where many of the trees still come from wild stands. Plantation-grown Douglas fir is steadily increasing its share of the market there, however.

Firs

At a distance the layman often confuses the spruces and firs because their forms are so similar. The best way to tell them apart is to examine the needles. The needles of fir trees are longer than spruce needles and not so stiff. Moreover, they are flat—two-sided rather than four-sided like the spruces—and less pointed.

Balsam fir. This species occurs naturally in Canada from Ontario to the Labrador Peninsula and the Maritime Provinces. In the United States, it is found in northern Minnesota, Wisconsin, Michigan, New York, and New England, on low, swampy land. From western Massachusetts and central New York south to southwestern Virginia, it grows in the high Appalachian Mountains on well-drained, moist soils.

Balsam fir is one of the best sellers on the market, perhaps because of its pleasing fragrance. Its needles are a rich green and vary from about one-half to one inch in length. Freshly cut trees retain their needles well in warm, dry rooms during the holiday period; but trees cut several weeks before use and shipped long distances lose their needles early under normal room conditions.

Although many balsam fir trees reaching the Christmas-tree markets still come from wild land, the number planted is increasing, especially in New England, New York, Pennsylvania, and the Lake States. Plantings should be made in moist, well-drained soils on protected, cool slopes.

White fir. White fir occurs naturally from northern Oregon, southward through the mountains of California, New Mexico, southern Colorado, and Arizona into northern Mexico. It is a popular Christmas-tree species in the western states.

30

Its qualities are excellent for Christmas-tree use. Needles range from about one to two inches in length and are a dull, blue green in color. Growth is slow; twelve to twenty years are required to produce the desired sizes.

Planting sites for this tree should have moist, well-drained soil. Best survival and growth occur in cool climates.

Other firs. Several other firs native to the Northwest make up nearly 10 percent of the Christmas trees planted there. Grand fir, popular in many areas, is the most easily grown in plantations. Noble fir and Shasta red fir, both high-altitude species and slow growers, have been grown successfully in a few low-elevation plantations west of the Cascades. Another recent "comer" is Fraser fir, indigenous to high elevations in the southern Appalachians. Even handsomer than its northern cousin, balsam fir, Fraser fir commands a premium price in some markets.

Other Species

Eastern redcedar. This species (not a true cedar but one of the junipers) occurs naturally in nearly all the states east of the Great Plains, but is planted and used for Christmas trees mostly in the southeastern states. Farther north, in the cooler autumn temperatures, the foliage often develops a purple bronze color about harvest time, a fact which makes it less desirable for Christmas use. Hence the trees are generally cut and sold in their native locality.

Eastern redcedar has many good qualities. Its symmetry is good and its deep green foliage dense. The chief objectionable feature is its sharp, stiff needles that make handling and decorating somewhat unpleasant. The needles are one-half to three-fourths inch long. It will survive and grow in a wide range of soil and moisture conditions, but does best on moist, well-drained, alkaline soils. Redcedar is a slow grower, however, taking as long as ten years to reach salable size.

Species to Grow

Arizona cypress. The range of this tree is chiefly in Arizona and western New Mexico. It resembles the eastern redcedar in form but has a dense blue green foliage of needles about one-sixteenth inch long that are less pointed than those of redcedar, making the tree easier to handle.

Arizona cypress is gaining favor in the southeastern states for Christmas-tree plantations. Its natural form is somewhat too columnar, but it can be shaped easily by frequent shearing.

Although the species grows naturally on dry, unfertile soils, plantings should be made on moist, well-drained soils for good growth. Application of fertilizer has increased growth and vigor of trees planted on poor soils. Under good conditions, salable trees can be produced in four years.

4

WHERE TO GET TREES

One of the things that the beginner most commonly asks is, "Where and how can I get trees to plant?" Selecting the source and kinds of trees to grow is a decision next in importance only to selecting the planting site and species. If you start out with good, sturdy, well-developed trees of species that are suited to your climate and site, you are well on the way toward success in your Christmas-tree business.

If you could scatter seed on your land to start your plantation, it would be much easier and cheaper than planting seedling trees. But many years of experience in reforestation work have shown that direct seeding is a risky business at best. In the long run it has proved to be much less sure and often much more expensive than planting seedling trees. Even planted seedlings a couple of years old and several inches high sometimes fight a losing battle with the weather and natural vegetation. The chances that a seed will germinate, survive, and grow satisfactorily under field conditions are slim indeed. That is why most, if not all, serious Christmas-tree growers start out with young trees and not seed.

There are three possible sources of young trees, or planting stock, as it is called: you can dig them up from wild land; you can grow them from seed in your own nursery; or you can buy them from professional nurseries.

The first two sources are of negligible importance in the Christmas-tree business. Transplanting seedlings from a forest environment to a plantation is a costly, time-consuming job. In some places, chiefly in the eastern provinces of Canada where there are ample supplies of natural tree seedlings, collecting and replanting these "wildlings" is practiced on a small scale. This is done mostly by operators of small Christmas-tree farms; very few of the larger operations take advantage of this source.

There are at least two good reasons for not recommending the practice. First, the cost of collecting usually exceeds the cost of nursery-grown trees. And second, the root systems of wildlings are long and stringy, not compact and fibrous like the roots of nursery stock. As a result, survival of transplanted wildlings is usually very poor.

The idea of growing trees from seed in his own nursery appeals to many a beginner, but the successful operation of a nursery of any size is a job for a specialist. It is an art and a science in itself, subject to many hazards that the amateur would find discouraging. The prospective, inexperienced grower is far better advised to do as most growers do and buy his planting stock from professional nurseries. In the long run this is the cheapest and easiest way to get good trees. Nearly all young trees set out in Christmas-tree plantations are grown from seed in nurseries. The Christmas-tree grower buys his trees from the nursery, usually when they are from one to four years old.

PUBLIC NURSERIES

Many states and some Canadian provinces operate nurseries that produce seedlings for reforestation. Some of these agencies will sell (or give) stock to Christmas-tree growers. They reason that a Christmas-tree farm is a "forest" and it is their duty to encourage the planting of new forests, regardless of the ultimate motive of the land-owner. The states that do not sell to the Christmas-tree farmer feel that they should produce seedlings only for re-forestation purposes and that they should not compete with the commercial nurseries in producing Christmas-tree stock. The states and provinces that do supply Christmas-tree stock usually sell seedlings at about the cost of production. So if you happen to live where such stock is available, you are in a position to get fairly good trees at a very reasonable cost. To find out the policy in your locality, contact the office of your state or provincial forester.

Publicly owned nurseries, however, have only a limited supply of stock available each year for private use. Moreover, since their primary purpose is to produce planting stock for reforestation, the trees they produce are intended chiefly for timber production and not for Christmas trees. Consequently, the Christmas-tree grower cannot always get the species and quality of trees he wants. So, in general, it is probably best not to depend upon public nurseries for your planting stock; the chances are you will be buying your stock from a commercial nursery (*Fig. 10*).

Figure 10. Pine seedlings in a nursery, ready for lifting. (*University of Minnesota, Agricultural Extension Service*)

COMMERCIAL NURSERIES

There are many reputable commercial nurseries throughout the country to choose from. Some of them, in response to the ever-increasing interest in Christmas-tree growing, have gaged their production to meet the demand for such stock. They obtain seed from the best varieties and strains available of the species in demand, both from North America and Europe. Some now specialize in Christmas-tree stock in addition to their regular landscaping stock. And some produce Christmas-tree stock exclusively. All this is good news, of course, because it means that you can obtain quality stock of any species that you choose, produced especially for your purpose.

SELECTING A NURSERY

The first consideration is quality of stock produced. Naturally the beginner wants to deal with a firm that handles high-grade trees; he does not want to be handicapped from the start with poor planting stock of questionable origin that has been carelessly produced. Any money saved at the outset by investment in such trees will be lost many times over in terms of low survival, poor development, and a discouraging number of unmarketable trees.

The care that the nurseryman gives to the trees when lifting them from the seedbed and packing them for shipment is almost as important as the quality of the trees themselves. So be sure that the nursery you select will give your stock the careful handling it deserves. Quality stock and careful handling, however, usually go hand in hand, so doing business with a reputable nursery almost ensures both.

Another thing that may influence your selection of a nursery is its location. Find one as near to your planting site as possible. Locally grown planting stock is less likely to suffer injury during shipment and is probably more readily adaptable to your site than stock from a more remote source. Lacking a local nursery, however, do not hesitate to order stock from a nursery several hundred miles away. But, if possible, select a nursery that is in a climate similar to yours. Trees from a nursery far to the north or south may not survive the shock of being moved as well as those grown in a climate more nearly like yours.

It might be a good idea during the first few years of planting to experiment with stock from several different nurseries—shop around a bit. In this way it is possible to find a nursery that produces the kind and quality of trees you want, gets them to you in good condition, at the proper time, and all for a fair price. You will also learn which of the different varieties of species handled by various nurseries do best on your site. There is sometimes as much difference in growth characteristics between two varieties of the same species as there is among various species. In other words, two varieties of Scotch pine may be different in color, vigor, drought resistance, and susceptibility to disease even though botanically they are the same species. As a result, you may get a shipment of Scotch pine from one nursery that does very well and a shipment of the same species (but a different variety) from another that is not satisfactory. Most growers have such an experience at one time or another, but by careful selection of species and varieties and by profiting from the experiences of others, it is possible to avoid most of these costly mistakes.

Tree geneticists are constantly working to develop new strains and hybrids specifically for Christmas-tree use. One positive result of this research is the establishment of seed orchards where trees having the inherent characteristics desired for Christmas trees are grown to maturity to serve as future sources for seed. The better nurseries keep close tab on such developments and obtain their seed accordingly; some of the larger ones even maintain their own seed orchards.

The best way to locate a reliable nursery is to consult local Christmas-tree growers, your county agent, or your extension forester. Also, check the advertisements in such reputable trade magazines as the *American Christmas Tree Journal* and the *American Nurseryman*. (These magazines are discussed further in the final chapter.)

5

CHOOSING THE PLANTING STOCK

When you have selected the species and varieties of trees you want to plant and have received catalogs and price lists from the nursery or nurseries you want to deal with, you are ready to order your trees. If you are a beginner, you should visit a nursery and make your selection on the ground. Then you can see what you are buying and benefit from the experience and advice of the nurseryman. Most veteran growers, however, find it neither convenient nor necessary to place their orders in person. Experience has taught them what, when, how, and where to order, and they generally do it by mail.

As you leaf through a nursery catalog, you will find that within a given species and variety there may be several different ages and sizes to choose from. You may buy trees ranging from one to four or more years old, and in size from three to ten or more inches high. (Height is measured from the ground line to the top of the tree; length of roots is not included.)

Age and size obviously are closely related; the older a tree is, the taller it is. However, the age-size ratio varies among species because some species naturally grow faster than others. For example, the pines in general grow faster than the spruces or firs. Moreover, the ratio often varies within a species because of differences in climate and local growing conditions. For example, a Scotch pine seedling in Minnesota may take a year or two longer to grow to a certain height than a similar tree in Ohio because of the shorter growing season farther north. Also, one of two nurseries in a certain locality may produce trees of plant-able size in two years, whereas the other nursery may take four years to produce similar stock, all because of differences in soils or nursery practice. Size, then, is more important to consider than age. Given a choice, buy your stock from the nursery nearest you that produces trees of the size you need in the shortest time. In this way, you are more likely to get thrifty stock that will do well in your own plantation.

TWO KINDS OF PLANTING STOCK

Nurserymen separate tree planting stock into two classes: seedlings and transplants. Seedlings are young trees that have not been moved from the seedbeds in which they germinated. They have not been disturbed at all except perhaps for weeding or thinning. Transplants are trees that have been lifted from their original seedbeds and re-planted elsewhere in the nursery. Thus, transplants are older, larger, and more expensive than seedlings.

In order to show the grower just what he is getting, the total age of planting stock is broken down into a two-digit figure: the first digit shows how long the young trees re-mained in the original seedbed and the second digit shows if and how long they were in the transplant bed. The sum of the two digits is the total age of the tree. For example, 2–0 indicates a two-year-old seedling; 2–2 indicates a four-year-old transplant that was left in the seedbed for two years and then moved to a transplant bed for two more years. As you can readily see, the second digit is the key to the identity of the stock: a zero for the second digit indi-cates a seedling; a whole number indicates a transplant.

Most planting stock ranges in age from two to four years, the most common age classes being 2–0 and 3–0 seedlings and 2–1 and 2–2 transplants (*Fig. 11*). Some 1–0 and 4–0 seedlings are used as well as some of the larger 2–3 and

Figure 11. 2–0 red pine seedlings. (*U. S. Forest Service*)

3–2 transplants. But, in general, the one-year-old seedlings are too small to plant by the usual methods and probably would have low survival anyway. And the five-year-old transplants are generally too large to plant easily and too expensive to buy.

What is the difference between a 4–0 seedling and a 2–2 transplant since both are four years old? In other words, what are the advantages of transplants over seedlings? First, there is the matter of size. Transplants are larger and sturdier than seedlings of the same age. This is because seeds are sowed very close together in the beds, usually less than an inch apart in the rows. By the time they are a year or two old they are beginning to crowd one another. Prolonged beyond two years, this competition tends to retard development of the seedlings, so the nurseryman moves them to larger quarters where they will have more room to grow. Thus a 2–2 transplant that has been growing for two years under relatively uncrowded conditions is more than likely a larger, sturdier tree than a 4–0 seedling that has been left in a cramped seedbed all its life. Under some planting conditions there is a distinct advantage to these larger-size trees.

In addition to being larger, transplants have usually developed more woodiness than seedlings. This also makes them more hardy and less easily injured. The smaller, more succulent seedlings are less apt to survive the rigors of a poor site or a dry planting season.

And finally, transplants usually have larger, better root systems—more fibrous and compact—than do seedlings. A newly planted tree transpires a lot of water, and unless it has a large root surface in close contact with the soil, it will not be able to absorb water fast enough to replace that which is lost through the needles. As a result, the tree will die. Lack of moisture, in fact, accounts for a great deal of the mortality in plantations during the first year.

Seedlings or Transplants?

Until recently, 2–0 seedlings were preferred by a majority of growers. Indeed, perhaps most of the successful plantations already established were started with 2-year-old seedlings. And, under average to better conditions, they still may be a good bet. But there is a marked shift toward more use of transplants in an effort to minimize the inevitable risk involved in getting a plantation "off the ground."

Transplants are more expensive to buy, but they may be cheaper in the long run.

To be sure, it is good business to buy the smallest stock that will suit your planting and growing conditions, but it is best to err on the large side. Three things will influence your decision: planting method, ground cover, and site.

The planting method you are going to use will influence the size of trees you should buy. Planting methods will be discussed in detail in Chapter 11, but in general, for hand planting, it is easier to use small trees (less than eight inches high) and for machine planting, larger stock is best (eight to ten inches).

If the ground cover on your land is low and sparse, you can use the smaller-size trees. But if the natural vegetation is tall and dense, invest in larger stock so that the trees will not be overtopped and shaded out by the surrounding plants. If your site is poorer than average, or if it is on a slope that faces south or west, or if it straddles a high, dry ridge, you had better seriously consider transplants as against seedlings. For average or better field conditions, 2−0 seedlings still will be an acceptable choice. By *average* or *better* we mean fairly good soil, well drained but not dry, and sparse to moderate ground cover (grass and weeds). Of course, 1–0 seedlings are cheaper, but in addition to being rather difficult to plant because of their small size, survival rate for these tiny trees under anything but the optimum field conditions is likely to be low. And trees that die the first year will have to be replanted the next year. So, buying trees too small for good survival is false economy.

Containerized Seedlings

An innovation in the tree nursery business that has caught on in the last several years is the development of "containerized" seedlings. Briefly, this is the production of seedlings in individual containers made of peat, paper, or plastic material (*Fig. 12*). The containers themselves are then planted in the field—without disturbing the roots of the seedlings. Such a system could have several obvious advantages. Because the seedling's growth and development are not interrupted as in normal transplanting, planting can be done anytime from spring through fall and not just during a two- to three-week period in early spring. For the same reason, plantable seedlings can be produced in a year or less. Moreover, the controlled environment inside the container, fertilized with just the right nutrients and

Figure 12. Containerized seedlings. Each container holds one seedling ready for planting. (*U. S. Forest Service*)

perhaps sterilized against disease, should give the seedling a head start during its first year or two in the field.

Although containerized seedlings are now used by many growers, there are still a few wrinkles to be ironed out. So far, seedlings in containers are expensive to produce. And, because they take up more space than bundled seedlings, they are expensive and inconvenient to transport and plant, although mechanical planters will eventually solve the latter problem. Another disadvantage is the small size of the seedlings, which may be smothered by falling leaves or crowded out by other vegetation. And finally, cramping of the roots until the container disintegrates could also slow early growth of the seedling.

How common this system becomes in the Christmas-tree industry during the next few years depends on how quickly and well these problems are solved. At any rate, the alert grower should be aware of its potential.

QUALITY AND PRICES

Quality or grade is also an important consideration. Unfortunately, some of the planting-stock grading systems are somewhat unwieldy to apply, especially for the inexperienced grower. But if you have some knowledge of the factors that are considered in grading stock and what constitutes a good tree, you should have little difficulty in selecting the grade of trees that you need.

A good tree is a sturdy tree and a well-balanced tree. More specifically, it is a tree that has developed some woodiness in its stem; it is not succulent and tender. It has a well-branched, fibrous root system that is at least as large as the top of the tree (i.e., the part above the ground). And, finally, a good tree has a stem relatively thick in relation to its length. Toothpick-thin stems should be avoided, regardless of the height of the tree.

The next consideration is prices. How much are you going to have to pay for your stock? Naturally, you want to buy trees suitable for your purpose at the lowest possible cost. On the other hand, you do not want to jeopardize the success of your enterprise at the outset by buying stock that does not meet the standards that your growing conditions require.

Prices for planting stock vary according to species, age, size, and quality. The older, larger, better trees, of course, command the highest prices. Obviously it costs the nurseryman more to produce 3–0 stock than 1–0 or 2–0 stock because of the additional time it has been under his care. Moreover, it costs more to produce 2–1 transplants than 3–0 seedlings because of the added cost of transplanting. And, of course, you must pay extra for the superior strains and better care that result in the highest quality stock.

Christmas-tree planting stock is usually priced and sold by the thousand. Here is a sample price list, giving some idea of the differences in price between seedlings and transplants and the range in prices to be found within a certain age:

	Price range per 1,000 trees
Seedlings	
2–0	$60–$120
3–0	$70–$140
Transplants	
2–1	$225–$425
2–2	$450–$550

Buying planting stock is not the biggest investment to be made, but it is one of the most important. It will cost more to plant and care for the trees than it will to buy them. A wise selection here will get your Christmas-tree business off to a good start; a critical mistake will not only waste the cost of the trees themselves, but also the time, labor, and money spent during the six to eight years necessary to produce a merchantable crop. The decision need not be a formidable one, however, if careful consideration is given to all the points discussed in this chapter.

6

PREPARING THE GROUND

Once the planting site is chosen and the trees ordered, the next problem is what to do about preparing the ground. The kind and amount of ground preparation needed will vary with the individual site. But if you know what ground conditions warrant the several treatments, you should have no trouble deciding what is best for your particular site.

The main purpose in preparing the ground before planting is to assure good survival and shape of the trees, *not to stimulate rapid growth.* Two things that greatly influence survival and form of planted trees are: condition of the soil, and amount and kind of natural vegetation present.

CONDITION OF THE SOIL

Of the two, the condition of the soil is the less important to the Christmas-tree grower because coniferous trees will thrive in a wider range of soil conditions than will farm crops. Hence, most soils that have been tilled or pastured are good enough for growing Christmas trees.

Extremes in soil fertility, however, are to be avoided. The fast growth of a "too fertile" soil can be offset by shearing (see chapter 13) and a slightly acid soil can be improved by liming. Soils too low in fertility should be tested to assess need for lime or fertilizer.

Extremes in texture are undesirable too. Soils that are so loose and sandy that they cannot hold water are just as bad as tight, heavy clays that are poorly drained. The best way to get favorable soil conditions is to select a site that has them in the first place.

NATURAL VEGETATION

Natural vegetation can be harmful to newly planted trees in two ways: first, a heavy mat of low, herbaceous plants such as grass and weeds can rob the young trees of soil moisture and nutrients. This is especially true if dry periods occur during the first year or two after planting. A tree that survives those first two critical years is usually well enough established to compete successfully with the grasses and forbs.

The low, herbaceous vegetation may deprive your seedling trees of water and essential minerals; the taller, woody plants deprive them of light. Brush or small trees may shade one side of a seedling planted nearby so that side does not develop as rapidly as the other. This of course results in a lopsided tree that is not marketable (*Fig. 13*). Moreover, if this overtopping vegetation is tall enough and dense enough, it can shade the young trees out entirely and cause them to die.

Some species of Christmas trees are more susceptible to such damage than others. The pines, for example, are more apt to suffer from shade than the spruces. Among the pines themselves, white pine is better able to withstand shade than any of the others. Therefore the kind of ground preparation needed depends chiefly upon the kind and amount of natural vegetation present. Let us consider each of the three main kinds of vegetational cover that are likely to be encountered.

Old Fields

Some planting sites need no preparation at all. These include old fields covered sparsely with grass or herbaceous plants, and recently cultivated fields with stubble from the last crop remaining. A field completely bare of any vegetation at all makes for easy planting, but such land is subject to erosion during the spring, summer, and fall, and to frost heaving during the early spring. Therefore

Figure 13. A red pine rendered completely worthless as a Christmas tree by shading from the clump of brush on the left.

it is better to have a light, low cover of some kind, whether it be new grass or old stubble (*Fig. 4*). Such sites, however, although they need no treatment before planting, are subject to rank weed growth and may require some vegetation control after planting.

If their land is suitable for farm crops, some growers like to prepare the site for planting a year ahead by growing a crop of wheat or other small grain in which a small amount of grass seed has been mixed. The following spring the soil is usually friable and protected from excessive surface erosion by the grain stubble and light grass cover. Soils thus prepared are in good condition for using a mechanical planter. Such ground cover is too sparse to damage trees and yet dense enough to protect and stabilize the soil.

Heavy Sod

Sites covered with a heavy sod need some preparation before being planted. This can be done by the use of herbicides, some kind of tillage, or a combination of both.

The use of herbicides by Christmas tree growers has greatly increased in recent years as more effective and selective products have been developed. Many kinds of chemicals are now available for killing grasses and herbaceous and woody plants, but great caution must be exercised in selecting and using them.

One of the best herbicides currently available for Christmas tree plantations is glyphosate (Roundup). It controls most annual and perennial weeds and grasses and some woody plants.

One method of treatment is to broadcast spray the entire area to be planted. This should be done in late summer or fall the year before planting is to be done. Such treatment will kill most of the weeds but still leave a mat of vegetation to protect the site against erosion. Woody plants should be cut off flush with the ground and the stumps treated with an

Figure 14. Under certain circumstances, it may be necessary to plow and disk the site before planting. (*Oregon State University, Extension Service*)

appropriate herbicide. To complete the job, the site is usually treated the following spring with a preemergence herbicide (one that attacks seeds, dormant buds, and roots).

Another way to eliminate heavy sod before planting is to apply an appropriate herbicide in narrow bands across the field at intervals equal to the intended spacing of the trees. Bands should be two to three feet wide and treatment should be done the summer before planting. Depending on the area to be planted and the equipment available, spraying can be done by hand or machine.

Laws regulating the use of herbicides differ from state to state and new ones are being passed each year. In some states, certain herbicides are banned altogether; in others, their use is restricted to specific areas and situations. For example, the use of certain herbicides is commonly forbidden near lakes, ponds, streams, homes, recreation areas, and food crops intended for human consumption. So, con-

Figure 15. Mechanical planters make the job easier and faster and are almost essential for planting large areas. *(University of Minnesota, Agricultural Extension Service)*

sult your local county agent or extension forester before considering the use of any chemical.

If your Christmas-tree farm is located in one of these restricted zones and you have a large area covered with heavy sod that is to be planted by hand, you might want to plow and disk or harrow the fall or spring before planting (*Fig. 14*). This can be costly and has some disadvantages, such as exposing the soil to wind and water erosion and making the planted trees more susceptible to frost heaving. But it will make the planting job easier and eliminate or at least slow down grass and forb competition for that first critical year or two. In any case, this method should only be used as a last resort.

Brushy Land

If the land is covered with brush and/or small trees, it must be cleared before planting. The best way to do this is to kill such vegetation with herbicides before or immediately after planting. It is almost useless to try to remove woody plants by cutting them because nearly all of them sprout prolifically, thus creating an endless maintenance job of cutting and recutting year after year. Land can be cleared with a bulldozer, but this is expensive and disturbs the soil excessively. Fire should never be used in any land-clearing operation. In the first place, it is hazardous to use. There is always a chance that a "controlled" fire will escape beyond its intended limits and destroy valuable cover, crops, or property on adjacent land. Moreover, fire consumes the organic matter on or near the surface of the ground, thus robbing the soil of some of its fertility. And, finally, fire only temporarily eliminates the unwanted vegetation. The roots of perennial plants are very rarely damaged by fire; hence the next year after burning, these plants will sprout up again more prolifically than ever.

The common chemicals used to kill woody plants are called *brush killers*. They may be applied either to the foliage or to the base of the tree or shrub. The latter is probably the best, easiest, and cheapest method because foliage sprays must be applied to both sides of the leaves, they generally take more herbicide per plant, and (if highly toxic chemicals are used) they are more dangerous to the operator and to nearby plants and animals because of the drifting vapor.

If only an acre or two at one time is to be cleared and planted, the job can be done with a back pressure sprayer, or even with a paint brush. But when several acres need to be treated, you may find it best to resort to a truck-mounted, motor-driven pressure sprayer. Such equipment is usually used to spray foliage only, and it must be used carefully to prevent damage to plants and animals in adjacent areas. If wind direction and velocity are taken into consideration, however, before spraying is begun, these factors can be used to advantage in getting quick, effective coverage of the intended area. Here again, be sure you know and adhere to the laws regulating the use of this type of herbicide in your area. And be sure to read and carefully follow the instructions for its use.

On land where it is practical to use farm machinery, you would do well to consider using a mechanical planter, especially if you are going to plant ten thousand or more trees at one time. There are several such machines on the market, all of which can be pulled behind an ordinary farm tractor (*Fig. 15*). Most of these planters prepare a foot-wide strip down each row of planted trees by destroying dense cover and loosening the soil. Their use makes special ground preparation unnecessary even in the densest ground covers.

GENERAL CONSIDERATIONS

Do not make any ground preparation that will lay bare the soil around the planted trees for long periods in regions where winter or spring freezing and thawing are common. Alternate freezing and thawing gradually lifts the planted trees from the ground, often killing them. Fall-planted trees are more subject to such injury than spring-planted trees, although spring-planted trees may heave during the second spring if not protected by some litter or good root growth.

When deciding how to prepare your land before planting, always keep this one important thought in mind: the main objective is to produce the most good trees as cheaply as possible. So do not undertake any treatment that will not more than pay for itself in good survival and growth of the trees. You cannot expect all the trees you plant to live. If no more than 5 or 10 percent of them die during the first two years, the planting operation can be considered a success.

7

WHEN TO
PLANT TREES

There is a right time and a wrong time to plant Christmas trees. If you should happen to plant yours at the wrong time—during the wrong season or when the soil condition is wrong—you stand to lose many of them before the first year is out.

The most critical period for tree survival is the first few months after planting—the period of adjustment to the new environment. If young trees can survive until the spring following planting, they are over the hump and will probably grow into salable trees. The grower, then, should do his planting at a time when weather and soil conditions during and immediately following planting will be favorable for good survival.

SPRING PLANTING

In general, there are two planting seasons: spring and fall. Spring is by far the more popular among growers because during the spring soil and weather conditions are likely to be best. Moreover, it is usually considered the most practical and convenient time to plant. By *spring* we mean any time after the last heavy frost and before the beginning of high daytime temperatures. Within this rather wide span of generally good weather, you should select a time for planting when the soil conditions are best. More about this later.

In the northern states and Canada, the spring planting

season may not begin until the latter part of May or early June; farther south it may begin as early as February 1. At any rate, you must fit your planting schedule to your climate.

The safe planting period may last from two to three months, so do not rush the season. This warning is particularly applicable to growers who live in the cooler climates. Overeager growers in the North sometimes begin planting before the last snow has melted. The result is heavy mortality among the trees that may have snow inadvertently packed around their roots. By the same token, do not wait too long. Trees planted during the hot summer months may die from drought or be choked out by competing vegetation before they even become settled in their new environment.

A good guide to the best seasonal time for planting is to select a week or two in midspring to do the job. If the beginner does not know exactly when this midseason occurs, he should consult other local Christmas-tree growers or nurserymen. He should make plans well in advance of the actual planting time, several months ahead if possible, in order to have plenty of time to get ready. This means, among other things, ordering planting stock early so that the nursery can schedule the shipment to arrive at planting time.

Another good reason for ordering planting stock early is that in recent years, as a result of the rapidly increasing interest in Christmas-tree growing, many nurseries have not been able to keep up with the demand for stock. Early orders are filled first and are most likely to contain the exact kinds of trees requested. Last-minute orders may have to be turned down because of lack of trees. More and more it is becoming a case of first come, first served.

FALL PLANTING

Some growers find it more convenient to plant in the fall. Although fall planting may often be fairly successful, it is not recommended because of the high mortality that is likely to occur.

Death of fall-planted trees may come about in either of two ways. In sections of the country where winter weather is changeable and snow lasts only a few days, alternate freezing and thawing of the soil has a heaving effect that often lifts the trees out of the soil, exposing almost the entire root system. This is more likely to occur on bare soils than on soils that have a moderately heavy cover of dead weeds or grass. Hence, if you do plant in the fall, do not expose the soil by plowing or scalping.

Winter killing is also common in areas where the soil remains frozen for long periods and the tops of the planted trees are exposed to wind. In such instances, death is caused by drought or desiccation because the roots cannot absorb water from the frozen soil as fast as it is evaporated from the needles.

In northern regions where snowfall comes early and remains on the ground throughout the winter, fall planting is less hazardous because the ground is soon covered with a blanket of snow that protects the newly planted trees and keeps the soil from freezing. Even in these regions, however, fall planting is not common.

Another drawback to fall planting is the difficulty of getting planting stock at that time. Most nurseries are geared to spring planting and schedule their stock lifting, packing, and shipping accordingly. They prefer to do this work only once a year; it would not be good business to make it a split-season operation. So, except for an unusually good customer, the average nurseryman would probably be rather reluctant to fill an order in the fall. The only alternative then would be for the grower to grow his own seedlings.

In the deep South, where the ground never freezes and winters are mild, the planting season is long, beginning with the late fall rains and lasting until late February or early March. The exact time of planting during this period is determined by the condition of the soil, the availability of planting stock, and the grower's own convenience.

Location of the nursery from which stock is ordered will also affect the exact time of planting. Local nurseries or nurseries located in a climate similar to the grower's will be able to ship stock in time for early or midseason planting. But if a grower in Ohio or Kentucky orders his stock from a Maine nursery, the lateness of the lifting season in the North may delay shipment as much as a month. Consequently, the planter must plan his work accordingly.

PLANTABLE SOIL

Assuming that you have decided to plant in the spring, you have selected a two- to three-week period in the middle of the planting season, and your stock has arrived: how do you decide the exact day to begin planting?

Plant when the soil is moist and friable. This usually means waiting until the spring rains are over and the soil has begun to dry out. If trees are planted when the soil is wet and sticky, the soil, upon drying, becomes hard and cakes around the roots, thereby preventing sufficient air and moisture from getting to the roots. This results in poor survival and growth.

Some of the heavier soils, such as clay, clay loam, and silty clay, tend to puddle when they become saturated with water during the frequent spring rains. These soils require a much longer drying period before they are plantable than do the lighter soils. Silty loams and sandy loams are not subject to harmful puddling and may be planted in a moister condition than soils that have a clay content of 10 to 15 percent or more.

A quick, reliable test of the moisture condition of a soil can be made by rubbing a pinch of it between thumb and finger or squeezing a handful into a ball. If it is sticky and puttylike, it is too wet for planting, and more time should be allowed for drying. Generally, if the soil is on the sandy side, it is safe to plant within a few days after a heavy rain. But if it contains a lot of clay, a heavy rain may delay planting a week or two or even more.

To sum up then, we recommend planting in the spring, after the soil has begun to dry out but while it is still moist, and before the grass and weeds have begun their vigorous spring growth. This is the safest, the most practical and convenient, and the pleasantest time to plant: safest because weather and soil conditions at this time are most conducive to good survival; the most practical and convenient because planting stock is more readily available in the spring and because the soil is workable and the natural vegetation sparse, making planting easy; and pleasantest because everyone likes to get out in the spring. Planting trees is one of the best spring tonics there is.

8

CARE AND HANDLING OF PLANTING STOCK

How to handle planting stock after it is received is of such importance to the survival and growth of the planted trees that we are devoting an entire chapter to the subject. Any part of the process of moving the young trees from the nursery to the plantation is potentially hazardous, but the growers themselves are usually responsible for any damage or mortality that occurs during this period. Almost no loss can be attributed to careless handling at the nurseries. Every reputable nurseryman knows that even a few losses in delivery for which he is responsible will hurt his business. So he takes every possible precaution to see that the trees get to the buyer promptly, safely, and in good condition. After being lifted from the beds, stock is usually kept in cold storage until time for shipping.

Shipment is usually by rail or truck express. But if the nursery is within reasonable driving distance from the planting site, you may prefer to transport your own trees by car or truck. Few trees are damaged today during long express hauls, especially if they are properly packed and are dormant at the time of shipment. The greatest danger lies in warm room storage at express terminals. But it can be said to their credit that express agents are becoming more and more aware of the need for promptly notifying the buyer when his shipment has arrived. Trees should be claimed immediately upon arrival.

STORING PLANTING STOCK

Once you have the trees in your possession, your main job is to keep them moist and cool until they are planted. If they become too warm or too dry they will die. What to do immediately upon receipt of the stock depends somewhat upon how many trees there are, how soon you will begin planting, and how long the planting will take. Begin planting as soon as you can after the trees arrive. In the meantime, there is a choice of three ways to handle the stock to keep it safe and fresh:

1. Put the stock in a cool place and water it. This method of handling is good if the amount of stock is small (say five thousand trees or less), if the trees are to be planted in the next three or four days, and if the weather is cool. The bundles may be placed on a north or east slope, protected from direct sunlight and covered with a tarpaulin; or they may be stored in a shed or barn. They should be loosened by cutting the binding cord or wire, or broken open if packed in crates, and watered once or twice a day. The small packages of trees (twenty-five or fifty to a bundle) should be stacked not more than two deep so that water and air can circulate freely around the roots. Trees respire and during the process they release carbon dioxide and heat. An accumulation of either in tightly packed bundles of trees can do much damage.

2. Place the trees in cold storage. If there is such a plant nearby, this is one of the best ways to store trees, especially if they must be kept for several days before planting or if the number is great enough to require several days to plant. Again, the bundles should not be stacked more than two deep. They should be kept at a temperature ranging from thirty to thirty-five degrees Fahrenheit. Trees should be removed as needed for planting, preferably a day's supply at a time.

3. Store the trees by heeling in. This is an effective way to keep trees in good condition for many days, but it means

extra work when large numbers are involved. To *heel in* trees, dig a V-shaped trench deep enough to accommodate the roots in a slanting position (*Fig. 16*). Loosen the trees from the bundles and spread them along the spade-cut wall of the trench so they are not stacked more than two or three deep. Then replace the soil and tamp it well against the roots. If the soil is not moist, water the roots before covering them with soil. If there are many trees, dig the trench as wide as necessary and place succeeding layers of trees

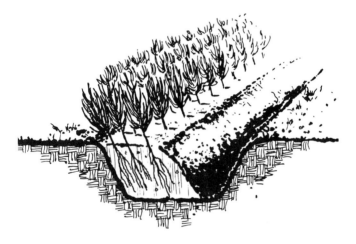

Figure 16. How trees are heeled in.

against the first, making sure to cover each layer with soil before starting the next.

Heeling in should be done near the planting site on a well-drained, protected area. The soil should be friable and easily worked. Trees should never be heeled in in a tight clay soil or where they will be flooded during rains, because the roots will become waterlogged. Also, to prevent early bud break, heeling in should only be done in cool weather.

The best assurance against loss is to plant the trees as soon after their arrival as possible.

CARE DURING PLANTING

The treatment that you give the trees after you remove them from storage until they are finally planted is just as important as the storage itself. Two things are involved: transporting the stock from the place of storage to the planting site, and handling the stock during the planting operation.

Consider first, transporting the stock to the planting site. Regardless of the distance, the bundles of trees, or loose trees, as the case may be, must be kept moist. Too often careless handlers throw the trees into an open truck and haul them miles to the planting site. During the entire trip the trees may be exposed to dry, fanning air, and later may be piled on the ground in the sunlight and exposed to the drying winds that are so common in springtime. Instead, trees should be thoroughly watered and covered in the truck with a tarpaulin or other protective cover and unloaded, if possible, in a shaded spot near where the planting is to be done.

It is important to keep the stock thoroughly moist throughout the entire planting operation. If trees are being planted by hand, they may be carried either in buckets or in planting trays (*Fig. 17*). If you use a bucket, sprinkle an inch or two of soil on the bottom and then half fill with water. If you use a planting tray, pack the roots of the trees in wet sphagnum moss or similar material and cover with well-moistened burlap.

Properly used, the tray is a better container because it will lie on slopes or rough ground surfaces without toppling over, a factor which helps to speed up planting. On the other hand, the bucket is generally safer in the hands of an inexperienced planter because it is easier to be sure that the roots are kept moist. In planting, one tree is removed from

Figure 17. Planting bucket and tray.

63

the tray or bucket at a time. Others may be pulled out of the moss or water inadvertently, however. If a tray is being used, the uncovered trees may go unnoticed until they are planted, during which time they may dry out. But if a bucket is used, the accidentally pulled trees usually fall back into the water.

It is just as important, of course, to keep trees moist if a mechanical planter is used. Such planters are equipped with metal trays into which buckets of trees can be placed.

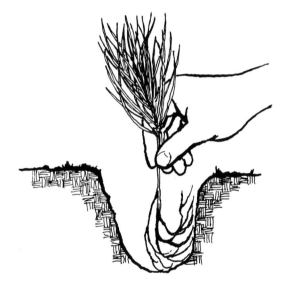

Figure 18. The roots of this tree are bent into an unnatural position that may retard the tree's growth. Avoid this by pruning the roots.

The importance of keeping the roots moist and protected at all times cannot be overemphasized. Failure to do this can result in greatly increased mortality of the trees during the first year. Experience has shown that exposing seedlings to sun and wind for as short a time as ten minutes is likely to

Figure 19. Pruning roots of seedlings to facilitate planting and avoid root deformity.

reduce survival by 10 percent. Leaving trees exposed to the weather for as long as two hours will result in two-thirds or more of them dying the first year. Moreover, those that do survive will be stunted in growth for several years.

ROOT PRUNING

Another precaution taken by many careful Christmas-tree growers to assure good survival is to prune the roots of the trees before planting. Most trees, especially seedlings, have roots much longer than the depth to which they are planted. Depending upon the size of the stock, trees are usually planted from six to eight inches deep. If a seedling's root system is longer than eight inches, the excess portion may be inadvertently doubled back as the tree is inserted into the planting slit or hole (*Fig. 18*). Especially long roots may even be left with their tips above the soil surface after planting. Such exposure to the air may well kill the seedling; and if the tree does survive, the contorted, unnatural

65

position of the roots will almost certainly retard its growth and development. Careful placing of all the roots in the hole will help survival. But doing this slows up planting. The answer is to prune the roots.

The best time to prune the roots is when the bundles of trees are opened preparatory to filling the buckets or planting trays. At the nursery, trees are generally sorted and tied into small bundles of twenty-five or fifty, according to size, which in turn are packed into the large bundles for shipment. At the planting site, you can quickly prune the roots to the desired length with a sharp knife or machete before you open small bundles (*Fig. 19*).

All the details of stock care described here may seem at first to be tedious and time-consuming to the beginner. But the several procedures involved soon become automatic with experience, and, if properly done, will pay dividends in time, money, and effort saved.

9

PLANNING AND MANAGING THE PLANTATION

A well-planned and well-managed Christmas-tree farm will yield some income to its owner every year after the first harvest. The idea, of course, is to plan the operation so as to have some merchantable trees ready to harvest each year. There are two general systems for attaining this end and several variations of each. The basic difference is that in one you plant your entire area the first year and in the other you plant only part of it.

THE ROTATION

Regardless of which system you use, the first step in setting it up is to decide upon a rotation. By *rotation* we mean the period between planting and harvesting—in other words, the number of years it takes to grow a salable tree.

It might seem to the beginner that the simplest way to determine the best rotation for his trees would be to plant some and then wait and see how long it takes them to reach merchantable size. In order to use the preferred system, however, it is important to know beforehand what the rotation is going to be. Following are some of the things that affect rotation:

In the first place, the number of years you leave the trees in the plantation is affected by the market. Regardless of whether the people in your section of the country favor small table-size trees or the larger floor models, their preference will influence your rotation. Select as your rotation the number of years it takes a tree to attain the average height preferred by your buyers. Fortunately, there is not a lot of variation throughout the country as far as size preference is concerned. For most markets six feet is a good standard height. Some people like them a little shorter; some favor taller ones. But if you establish as your rotation the number of years it would take the average tree in your plantation to reach six feet, the variation in growth rate among individual trees will provide you with a range in sizes that will satisfy even the most selective buyers.

Once you have familiarized yourself with the peculiarities of the market in your locality, you can turn your attention to growth rate; this is the most important factor affecting rotation. Growth rate, and hence rotation, varies by species, climate, and site. Extremes range from a two-year rotation for Monterey pine grown in California under cultivation and artificial watering to a twenty-year rotation for Douglas-fir in British Columbia. For most Christmas-tree species, however, rotation will range from six to ten years.

There is a great deal of variation in growth rate among species. For example, the true firs and the spruces, including Douglas-fir, grow much slower than do most of the pines. Hence, it takes several years longer for a Norway spruce to grow to merchantable size than it does an Austrian pine.

The natural impulse of the inexperienced grower is to buy the fastest-growing species he can get in order to reduce the rotation. Too rapid growth rate, however, is a serious detriment to quality. Trees that grow at a moderate, uniform rate are best. Development of fast-growing trees can be controlled by proper shearing, but this tends to lengthen the rotation. Nevertheless, shearing is a highly recommended cultural practice that will be discussed more fully in Chapter 13.

Climate or length of growing season also affects rotation.

In the North, or at high altitudes, where the growing season is short, growth rate for a given species is slower than farther south or at lower altitudes, where long growing seasons prevail.

And, finally, the site itself, the tree's immediate environment, influences growth rate. Good soil, proper moisture and light, and adequate drainage mean fast growth and a short rotation.

HOW A TREE GROWS

Reduced to simple terms, the typical evergreen tree consists of a vertical stem from which, at more or less regular intervals, groups of branches extend like spokes on a wheel. The branches are clothed with leaves or needles. Each group of branches is called a *whorl,* and most evergreen trees that are used for Christmas trees produce one whorl per year. The distance between whorls thus represents one year's height growth. At the end of each growing season a large bud called the *terminal bud* forms at the top of the stem. This is where the next year's vertical growth will begin. In addition, there are several lateral buds clustered below and around the terminal bud. In the spring the central stem will begin to grow upward again, and the several branches will begin to grow outward, forming a new whorl (*Fig. 20*). If a tree is permitted to grow too fast, the distance between whorls or groups of branches on some species is likely to be eighteen inches or more. So, instead of having a bushy full-bodied tree, you have one that looks like a skeleton.

Not all species, however, are limited to one whorl a year. Some of the southern pines—notably shortleaf, pitch, Virginia, and slash pine—produce two to four whorls in a growing season. Such species can be permitted and even encouraged to grow fast, because the distance between the whorls will seldom exceed twelve inches. Eastern redcedar is another southern species that can be grown rapidly because this species does not produce whorls at all. Instead it

Figure 20. Profile of a fast-growing pine. Arrows show current year's growth. Upper arrow points to terminal bud; lower one points to latest whorl.

develops branches profusely all along the stem, and so its growth rate has little effect upon the density of its foliage.

PLANTING THE ENTIRE AREA

Getting back to the two systems for planting, the simplest is to plant the entire area the first year, wait for the trees to grow to salable size, then cut them all for the current market, and replant the area the following spring. The chief disadvantage of this method is immediately apparent: your income comes only at the end of each rotation. In other words, if you are operating on a six-year rotation, you would be able to sell trees only three times in eighteen years. Needless to say, this is not good business. No matter which system you use, you will not be able to cash your first check from Christmas-tree sales until one rotation period has passed, but you certainly do not want to wait for another complete rotation to cash your second.

In order to get around this, some growers who use this system take advantage of the difference in growth rates among individual trees and harvest each tree as it reaches salable size. This spreads the cut and therefore the income over a two- to four-year period. The spots vacated by the harvested trees are replanted the next spring. The ultimate result, of course, is a plantation containing trees of all ages and sizes scattered haphazardly throughout the area. For a small plantation of an acre or two, this system may be satisfactory. But for a larger area, the job of maintenance and harvesting in such a mixed plantation becomes increasingly difficult and costly. The harvestable trees are scattered over the entire area. Each year they must be sought out, cut, and dragged individually to a concentration point for loading. The following spring the vacant spots left by the harvested trees must again be located and replanted. Shearing and protective treatments against insects and diseases also become proportionately slow and tedious because of the mixture of sizes. All this means money and time wasted, neither of which the serious Christmas-tree grower can afford. Another disadvantage to this system, particularly for the large grower, is that all replanting must be done by hand. This objection can be overcome, in part, by postponing replanting until nearly all the original trees have been harvested and then planting by machine between the original rows. But this means a costly delay in getting the second rotation started. In general, any rotation system that involves planting the entire area the first year is not recommended.

PLANTING BY BLOCKS

Most successful growers, whether they operate small or large Christmas-tree farms, follow one form or another of the block system of rotation. Under this system the entire tract of land to be devoted to Christmas-tree production is divided into blocks of equal size, the number corresponding to the grower's best estimate of the rotation age for his species. (Hence the need for determining the rotation before starting to plant.) Then one of these blocks is planted

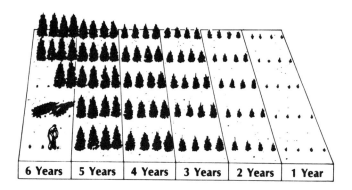

| 6 Years | 5 Years | 4 Years | 3 Years | 2 Years | 1 Year |

Figure 21. An idealized version of planting in blocks on a six-year rotation. At the stage shown, one block can be harvested and one block planted each year indefinitely.

each year until all have been planted. For example, suppose you have twelve acres of land and estimate that you can produce salable trees in six years. You would stake out six blocks of two acres each and plant one block the first year, another the second year, and so on. At the end of the sixth growing season, the first block is ready for harvesting and the land is now in full production. You will harvest and plant two acres of trees each year now for as long as you or your heirs care to stay in business (*Fig. 21*). Of course, the income from your first harvest will not be as high as if you had planted all the area the first year, but what is more important, beginning the sixth year you will be getting an income every year, instead of every six years.

Besides guaranteeing a steady, annual income, the block system has several other merits to recommend it: ground preparation work need only be done on that portion of the area to be planted that year; and only enough trees for one block need be bought and planted each year. Thus, you work and pay by installments instead of by the lump sum, thereby minimizing your annual expenditure of labor and money. This is especially helpful to the beginner, who is going to have his hands full personally, and perhaps financially, during the first year anyway. The advantages of block planting continue to accrue throughout the rotation. Mowing, spraying, and shearing can be done more easily and economically in small blocks containing trees of almost uniform size. And finally, the harvesting operation can be greatly simplified if all or nearly all the trees in a block can be cut at one time.

Theoretically all the trees in a given block should be ready to harvest at the end of the rotation period; but in practice this is usually not the case. Some of the trees, for one reason or another, may have lagged behind in growth, and others, although large enough for harvesting, are too poorly formed to be merchantable. There are then two alternatives: you can leave these trees in the plantation for another year or two, if you are reasonably sure they will develop into salable trees in that time; or you can cut the poorly formed trees to sell as greens and ball the smaller ones to sell to nurseries for landscaping. Balling is discussed in Chapter 18.

If you decide to leave them in the plantation, you can start the next rotation in that block by planting new stock in the spots from which trees were cut. Such planting will have to be done by hand, however, because the scattered remaining trees would interfere with a mechanical tree planter. Some growers prefer to plant the second crop of trees between the original rows. If this is done, and a mechanical planter is used, the need for plowing out the old stumps is eliminated. Moreover, planting the second crop between the rows allows you to do all the replanting on that block at once instead of waiting until the last of the first rotation trees are cut to fill in those vacant spots. The presence of the few older trees will not harm the newly planted ones during the year or two before the last of these first rotation trees are harvested.

Another modification of the block system practiced by some growers is to cut all the trees on a block when they have reached rotation age, regardless of age or form. Then, the next spring the block is plowed and seeded to wheat or oats mixed with grass or grass and red clover. The purpose of sandwiching a grain and grass crop between rotations is to prevent a cover of heavy sod or dense brush from developing on the site. Plowing and seeding with grain and grass results in a light cover that stabilizes the soil but does not interfere with young tree growth. This practice is usually limited to larger plantations where a single block runs to twenty acres or more and on sites that are good enough to make growing a crop of grain profitable.

The above discussion has been based on the assumption that you are going to plant only one species, or at most two species with similar growth rates.

It is often considered good business, however, to grow several different species. Such a practice provides the grower some insurance against changing markets and against complete loss if an insect infestation or disease epidemic should destroy or damage all the trees of one particular species. But it is not advisable to mix two or more species in a single plantation or block, especially if a fast-growing and a slow-growing species are included. Such a mixture will unnecessarily complicate maintenance, harvesting, and replanting operations. The accepted way to grow different species is to mix only those species that have similar growth rates and site requirements. Trees with different growth characteristics should be grown separately under separate rotation systems.

Operators of many of the big commercial tree farms in the northeastern states produce six to eight different kinds of Christmas trees having widely varying growth rates and site requirements to meet diversified markets. They manage nearly every species as a unit, however.

The block system works best on areas that have uniform site conditions. Growth on such sites is most likely to be uniform, making it possible to harvest and sell all the trees

Figure 22. New block being planted next to old one ready for harvest. (*University of Minnesota, Agricultural Extension Service*)

on a block at the same time. And uniform site conditions also mean that the growth rate will be about the same on all blocks, and hence the trees on each successive block will become harvestable on schedule.

If you have more than three or four acres to work with, we recommend that you divide it up into blocks and plant one block each year. Throughout the years this has proved to be the most practical system for raising Christmas trees and lends itself to the greatest economy of time and effort in the long run (*Fig. 22*).

10

SPACING OF TREES

There is one more thing to consider before actually starting to plant the trees—and that is spacing. The spacing of the trees (how far apart to plant them) can affect net monetary returns in two different ways: first, spacing determines how many trees can be planted per acre of ground; and second, spacing influences the growth and development of individual trees. To plant trees too far apart is not to make full use of the area available; and if planted too close together, they become stunted and deformed. In either case, your land is not producing at its maximum capacity—and you are losing money.

The ideal spacing, then, is that which allows the most trees to be planted per acre and yet gives each tree ample room to grow and develop without interference from its neighbors. This ideal spacing varies according to species and the size of trees you are planning to grow.

SPECIES AND SPACING

Some species need more room to grow than others, either because they are naturally more bushy or because they are less tolerant of shade. As a group, the pines need more elbowroom than the spruces and firs. In the first place, the market seems to demand that pines be broad in relation to their height, with a slightly rounded profile. Spruces and firs, on the other hand, should be more slender and have straight sides; their outline should be wedge-shaped (*Fig. 39*). Moreover, the pines are more susceptible to damage by shade than are most of the other Christmas-tree species. If they are shaded by other trees, the shaded branches are likely to starve and die, or their needles may turn yellow. In either case, the affected portions are made unfit for use. Most such damage occurs on the lower part of the tree, so in order to salvage the remainder for the market, the grower must cut it off high, perhaps two feet above the ground. This usually means a loss of two or three years' growth. The most severe damage is done if the branches of adjacent trees overlap. However, even if the tips of the branches of neighboring trees do not actually touch, too close spacing will affect the shape of the trees.

The spruces, firs, and cedars, being more columnar in shape and more tolerant to shade, can be planted closer together than the pines.

SIZE AND SPACING

The size of trees you intend to market will affect their spacing in the plantation. If you plan to grow small trees, you can plant them much closer together than if you plan to grow larger ones. The market itself will, of course, determine what size or sizes you should grow. In general, there are three different sizes of Christmas trees in demand: table size, floor size, and (for want of a better name) community or group size.

If you plan seriously to supply two or more of these different tree sizes, the best way to do it is to devote a certain amount of your total area to each size. Then you can space your trees accordingly—close together for the small-tree market, and farther apart for the large trees. Some growers attempt to grow all sizes on one area. Their plan is to start out with close plantings, and in two or three years as the trees grow and begin to crowd each other, to remove every second, third, or fourth one for the small-tree market, then, in a few more years, to make another thinning, heavier this time, for the floor-size market. The few remaining trees are then left to grow to the larger sizes, ten, twelve, or more feet, for the community-tree market.

This theory never works out very well in practice, however, because it is based on the assumption that all trees grow at the same rate. If this were true, it would then be possible to thin according to a definite pattern, making sure that each remaining tree had enough space to grow. But, as we have seen, trees do not grow at the same rate—not even trees of the same species, from the same source, and planted in the same ground. As a result, the grower trying to supply the various markets by thinnings finds that he must cut the trees that are ready to be cut, regardless of their location in the plantation. Minor differences in site quality from one side of his plantation to the other will be reflected in the rate of growth of the trees. Hence he may find that the trees in one spot are crowding each other more than those in another. This means that more drastic thinning is necessary in the denser parts and therefore an uneven distribution of the remaining trees is the result. After two or three thinnings, part of his land may be almost cleared of trees while other parts contain clumps of trees too close together to develop properly.

All this leads to a disorganized situation in which the grower never really knows how many trees he will have to sell in any one year. Moreover, he will be producing an unnecessary number of deformed, unmerchantable trees, many of which he will have to cut and destroy in order to relieve locally crowded conditions. And finally, harvesting only a fraction of the trees in a plantation at one time always increases the time, effort, and supervision needed. So it is best to establish a definite rotation for each block in the plantation and harvest all the trees at the end of that period. This will result in a wide enough range in sizes to satisfy most of the customers. But for extra small or extra large trees, we strongly recommend establishing separate blocks and spacing the trees accordingly.

Assuming that the grower wants to produce trees of all sizes for the various markets, what percentage of his area should have close spacing, medium spacing, and wide spacing? In other words, how many trees of each size should he plan for? The answer to this question, of course, depends upon the local market—what size trees do the people want?

Nine out of ten trees bought are used in private homes. And the preferred height for these trees is from five to seven and a half feet. Many trees taller than seven and a half feet are bought for home use, but these are usually cut off at the top or bottom to fit the room height. People who live in small homes or apartments usually buy smaller trees, ranging in height from three to five feet. In recent years the demand for these table models has been noticeably increasing.

A reasonable division for the grower to make in order to supply all these markets would be to plant 5 percent of his trees at a wide spacing (seven to eight feet apart), 85 percent at medium spacing (five to six feet apart) and 10 percent at close spacing (three to five feet). The long-needled pines (such as red pine) are best suited for medium and large trees. Spruces, firs, cedars, Scotch pine, and other short-needled pines are acceptable in all sizes, but are especially preferred for the table size.

To maintain a plantation in a reasonably productive condition, uniform distribution should be maintained. During the spring following the initial planting, blank spots where trees failed to survive should be replanted. This is a hand-planting job. Whether or not blanks created by the first and subsequent partial harvests are replanted depends upon the plan of the grower. If he intends to clearcut the whole block within two or three years, then he should not replant until all the first-rotation trees have been removed. This is considered the best way to manage a plantation, and is essential if machine planting is done. If the grower is planning to maintain a plantation of trees of all sizes, however, replanting of spaces left by dead and cut trees should be done each spring.

SPACING AND NUMBER

As mentioned before, the spacing of the trees determines the number that can be planted on an acre. Usually trees are spaced evenly in all directions, so that a 3 × 3 spacing means that the trees are planted every three feet in rows that are three feet apart. Following is a tabulation of the number of trees that can be grown on one acre at various spacings:

Spacing in feet	Number of trees per acre
3 × 3	4,840
4 × 4	2,722
5 × 5	1,740
6 × 6	1,210
7 × 7	890
8 × 8	680

Even a foot difference in spacing can account for so many trees that it pays to consider very carefully the spacing you are going to use before you begin to plant.

Unfortunately, no hard and fast rules for spacing can be laid down; however, standard spacing for trees to be grown to six or seven feet in height is usually about five or six feet. Pines should seldom, if ever, be planted closer together than this (except perhaps for growing very small trees); spruces and firs can be grown successfully at the closer spacings.

When planting is done by hand, it is rather difficult to maintain uniform spacing. Since this is important, however, you may want to take the extra time and effort to mark guidelines. Spacing in the rows is usually done by eye or by pacing, but if at the beginning you do not trust yourself to use either of these two methods, you can use your planting tool as a measuring stick. Although this takes extra time and effort, it can assure more precise spacing in both directions, which is important if you plan to use power equipment for mowing and cultivating. You might start out this way and then after you have planted two or three rows, guide yourself from then on by sighting back at the planted trees.

Many commercial planting machines have attachments that mark the planting spots with sawdust or lime. This results in a plantation in the form of a perfect grid or checkerboard and permits machine mowing in two directions (*Fig. 23*).

Figure 23. A well-spaced plantation. (*Oregon State University, Extension Service*)

SPACING AND COST

The cost per acre for establishing a plantation will vary with the spacing of the trees. Assuming a cost of 120 dollars per thousand trees for planting and 140 dollars per thousand for the stock itself, differences in total

cost among the various spacings commonly used are as
follows:

Spacing in feet	Planting cost ($120.00 per thousand)	Cost of stock ($140.00 per thousand)	Total cost per acre
3 × 3	$581	$678	$1,259
4 × 4	327	381	708
5 × 5	209	244	453
6 × 6	145	169	314
7 × 7	107	125	232
8 × 8	82	95	177

It would cost about four times as much to plant trees at a
3 × 3 spacing than at twice that (6 × 6). To these costs must
be added, of course, other incidental costs: transportation,
storage, ground preparation, tools, and so on. But at any
rate, the above table gives a conservative estimate of the
cost of planting trees. Of course, the more trees the more
harvest, so these costs should really be considered as an
investment rather than an expense.

11

THE PLANTING JOB

The fact that more than one-third of this book is taken up with merely getting ready (i.e., the planning and preparation phases) should certainly emphasize the importance of these preliminaries. More often than not, the success or failure of the Christmas-tree business will be determined by what is done in the early stages before a tree is even put into the ground. But when the time comes to start planting, how do you go about it?

There are two methods of planting; one is by hand and the other by machine. Hand planting involves using any of a number of hand tools to get the trees into the ground. Machine planting requires an especially designed tractor-drawn machine that prepares the planting trench and compacts the soil around the tree roots. Which method is best depends chiefly upon the size and the condition of the planting site.

Hand planting is the more versatile of the two methods; it can be used wherever trees will grow, no matter how steep and rough the land or how stony and stump-and-root-infested the soil. Machine planting, on the other hand, is limited to fairly level or rolling land and obstruction-free soil. Moreover, in order to make an investment in a mechanical tree planter pay, a great number of trees (at least ten thousand) must be planted each year.

So, assuming that you plan to start out in a modest way, we shall discuss hand planting first and in greatest detail. Even if you do convert eventually to machine planting, you will still have to do some filling in and replanting by hand, so it is important to know how to do it.

Regardless of which method you use, your objective is to put the trees into the ground as rapidly, efficiently, and economically as possible. However, if you try to work too fast, you will do a sloppy job of planting and risk losing a high percentage of trees. This will cost money. On the other hand, if you are overmethodical and treat each seedling as if it were a rare ornamental, the planting job will become tedious and time-consuming. This can also cost money. The proper balance between speed and efficiency will result in the greatest economy.

HAND PLANTING

There are two commonly accepted ways to plant by hand; they are called the *slit method* and the *hole method*. In the slit method, the trees are planted in vertical slits in the ground and the slits are closed with the planting tool or boot heel after the trees have been inserted. In the hole method, the trees are planted in holes dug by a mattock (grub hoe), spade, or shovel, much as ornamental trees or shrubs are planted in a yard.

The Slit Method

Slit planting can be done by any of several tools, the chief ones being the planting bar and the mattock. The planting bar is made entirely of steel or steel and iron. It consists of a long T-shaped handle fastened onto a blade about ten inches long and three inches wide that tapers from a thickness of about three-fourths of an inch at the top to a sharp edge at the bottom, or business end (*Fig. 24*). At the top of the blade is a footrest like that on the blade of a shovel. The handle may range from twenty-five to thirty inches long, depending upon the height and preference of the planter. These tools may be bought from suppliers of tree-planting equipment, or they may be custom made in a local machine shop.

To use the planting bar, grasp the handle with both hands, and press the blade vertically into the ground with your foot to the depth that you want the trees planted. With a quick forward and backward motion widen the slit into a narrow V-shape. Pick a tree from the bucket or tray with one hand and insert it into the slit. Next, insert the blade again into the ground, this time about two inches behind the first slit, then by first pulling the handle toward you and then pushing it away you will press the sides of the first slit against the roots of the tree and thereby seal the opening. Finally, insert the blade a third time about halfway in and an inch or two behind the second slit. A twist of the handle will loosen the soil adjacent to the second slit and let it fall

Figure 24. The planting bar is perhaps the easiest of the hand-planting tools to use.

down into the opening. Complete the job by pressing the loose soil into the second slit with the heel of your boot (*Fig. 25*). In closing the slit, it is important that you pull the handle toward you *first,* so as to close the bottom of the slit first. If you do it the other way around, you are likely to leave an air hole near the tips of the roots. And if all the roots are not in close contact with the soil, they cannot draw moisture from the soil. Such a condition will retard the tree's growth and may even kill it. This may sound like a complicated and involved procedure, but actually it can be done in less time than it takes to describe it. A round-pointed, long-handled shovel or tile spade can also be used for slit planting.

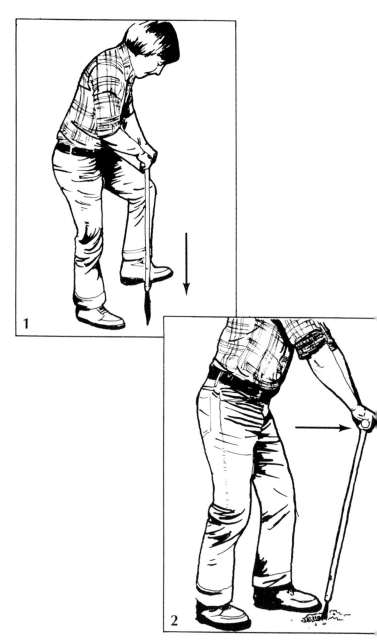

Figure 25. Steps in using the planting bar.

Figure 25 (continued)

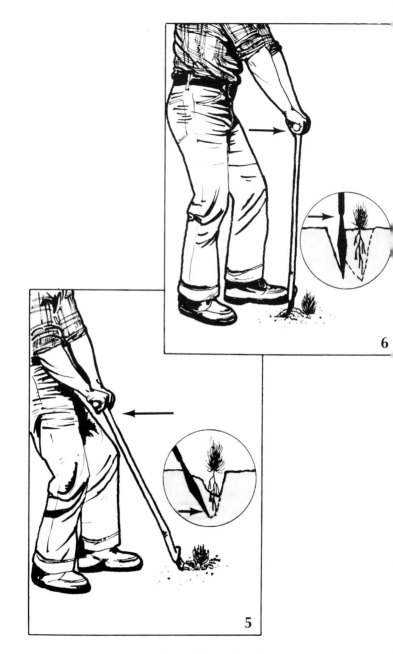

Figure 25 (continued)

Figure 25 (continued)

Although a planting bar is a specialized tool used only for planting trees, the mattock is a common tool that is known and used by most farmers and has many uses. It is probably best described as a hoe with a short, heavy, wooden handle and a long, heavy, steel blade (*Fig. 26*).

To use the mattock for slit planting, grasp the handle with both hands and drive the blade into the ground with a chopping motion. Widen the slit by pulling the mattock toward you with the handle parallel to the ground. While holding the soil back with the mattock in one hand, insert a tree into the slit with the other hand. Remove the mattock and finish the job by pressing the heel of your boot into the loosened soil (*Fig. 27*).

Figure 26. The mattock (or grub hoe) is the most versatile of the hand-planting tools.

The Hole Method

The holes can be dug with a narrow spade, a long-handled shovel, or a mattock. The mattock is the favored tool because it can do the job easier and faster than either of the other two. Spade and shovel planting are usually limited to small jobs or to light soils where it is easy to insert the blades into the ground. Planting is done simply by digging a hole deep enough to accommodate the roots of the tree, inserting the tree into the hole, and filling in around the roots with loose soil. A variation preferred by some planters is to dig the hole so that one side is vertical. Then

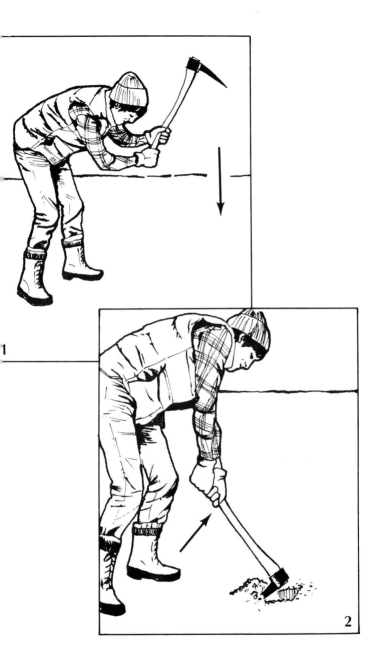

Figure 27. Steps in slit planting with the mattock.

3

4

Figure 27 (continued)

Figure 27 (continued)

place the seedling against the vertical side and fill in with loose soil. This side-hole method, although faster, results in one side of the root system being pressed against a wall of compacted soil, whereas in the center-hole method, the entire root system is surrounded by loose soil.

General Considerations

In selecting which planting tool and method to use, some compromise has to be made between what is easiest for the

93

planter and what is best for the trees. Certainly, planting each tree in the center of a hole so that the roots are completely surrounded by loose soil is best for the trees. And for maximum survival, regardless of time and effort involved, this is the way to plant. Planting in holes is a slow and laborious job, however, and most growers would rather use a more rapid, less painstaking method, even if it means risking a little greater mortality.

The fastest and least tiring hand-planting method is planting in slits with a bar. This technique is the easiest to master and requires less bending and stooping (*Fig. 28*). It is best adapted to sandy or loamy soils and to sites where the natural vegetation is sparse or where the site has been prepared by machine. In tight, clayey soils, the planting bar tends to puddle the soil around the roots, and it is hard to insert it into rocky soils. Because the bar makes a relatively small slit, small planting stock must be used with this tool.

For all around versatility, the mattock cannot be beat. It is useful under a wider range of conditions than any of the other hand-planting tools. It is the most practical and efficient tool to use in heavy, clay soils and in rocky soils. And on sites where there is a mat of sod so heavy and thick that scalping is necessary, the mattock is practically indispensable. No other tool can do this scalping job as efficiently. The mattock, however, is somewhat difficult to use properly. It is tiring to use because of the greater amount of energy required to drive the blade into the ground, and more stooping and bending are necessary. One of its chief advantages is that just about any size of stock can be planted with it.

Some growers object to slit planting because the roots of the trees are compressed into a single plane; that is, they are flattened instead of being spread out. They claim that this flattened position does not give the tree proper anchorage and support and that, as a result, the trees are more subject to drought and wind damage. In actual practice,

Figure 28. Business end of a planting bar. (*National Christmas Tree Association*)

however, this theory does not seem to be well enough founded to warrant abandoning the slit method. Many thousands of trees have been planted in slits throughout this country and Canada and elsewhere and have survived and developed normally.

Regardless of the method used, certain principles of planting must be observed to assure good survival and early growth. Ideally, the planted tree should be in an upright position with its roots extending downward and uniformly spread in the soil. The root crown, or the junction between the root and stem, should be at or slightly below the surface of the soil and the roots themselves should be in close contact with the soil. Here are a few hints that, if followed, will help you to attain or at least approach this ideal.

1. Spread the roots in the slit or hole as well as time will allow and make especially sure that the root system is not doubled back in a U-shape as is so often and so easily done.

2. Place the tree so that its root crown is slightly below the soil surface—not more than half an inch—so that when the soil has settled after the slit or hole has been closed or filled, the root crown will be in the same position that it was in the nursery bed.

3. Pack the soil firmly about the roots, keeping dead, dry leaves, grass, or other litter out of the hole.

4. Be sure that the soil around the tree is neither depressed in the form of a cup or raised in a hill. A tree planted in a depression is likely to drown when the depression fills with water. And one planted in a hill is likely to be drought killed because the water tends to run down the hill and away from the roots. It is also important that neither too much nor too little of the tree is exposed. The position of the root crown is the critical thing.

Although there may seem to be an overwhelming amount of dos, don'ts, and how-tos in this planting business, a little practice and experience in the method you select will give you all the skill and confidence you need. If you follow the directions and suggestions given here, you will soon be planting trees efficiently and almost automatically.

How fast can you plant by hand? Admittedly, compared with machine planting, hand planting is slow. The rate per man may vary, however, from three hundred to a thousand in an eight-hour day. Why such a wide range?

In the first place, the tool and planting method that you use affect planting rate. As was mentioned earlier, the fastest combination is planting in slits with a bar, and the slowest is planting in holes with a spade or shovel. Second, is the matter of soil and terrain. Regardless of the tool or method that you use, you will be able to plant faster if you have a light soil, such as a loam or sandy loam. As the soil becomes heavier and more rocky, your planting rate will slow down proportionately.

Rolling land is easier and faster to plant than level land. On such land it is best to plant uphill, although downhill planting is almost as fast if the planter faces uphill and walks backwards. The reason for this is obvious. If you do all your planting while facing uphill, the ground in front of you and hence the planting spot will be closer to you and easier to reach than on level ground. Slit planting with a mattock is especially well adapted to hilly terrain.

The right size of planting stock can also speed up your planting. Generally, six- to eight-inch seedlings or transplants are best for hand planting. Smaller stock is difficult to handle in sorting or separating in the bucket or tray and in inserting the flimsy root system into the planting slit or hole. This is especially true if the planter wears gloves, as many do. Larger stock, ten inches or longer, slows down planting because it is necessary to prepare larger slits or holes to accommodate the root system. Moreover, you cannot carry as many large trees as you can small ones, so the larger your stock, the more frequently you will have to interrupt your planting to replenish your supply of trees.

The kind and amount of ground cover influences planting time, as has been pointed out before. Of course, you could plant fastest if there were no ground cover at all and the bare mineral soil were exposed. Some ground cover is desirable, however, almost essential in fact, in order to prevent erosion and frost heaving. A light cover of grass is best, and this ideal can be attained if planting is done on a recently cultivated field, or if the site has been prepared a year in advance of planting. Ground-preparation practices are discussed in detail in Chapter 6.

Planting in heavy sod with no previous preparation is the slowest of all. On such sites, the vegetation must be scalped off of each planting spot, exposing a square foot or so of mineral soil in which to plant the tree (see *Fig. 14*). Under such conditions, there is no substitute for the mattock. This is the only tool commonly used for planting that will do an efficient job of both scalping and planting.

Finally, how fast and efficiently the trees get into the ground will depend upon the planters themselves. If you are doing all the planting yourself, you will want to learn to do a good job of planting and to do it as rapidly as possible. If you are going to have help, it is even more important that you yourself be a good planter, because you will probably have to train your laborers in the method you want them to use. Experience has shown that when hiring planters, it is best to get someone who has worked on a farm or in a nursery. Such people seem to have a special knack and feel for working with living plants.

MACHINE PLANTING

Machine planting is faster and easier than hand planting. Two men operating a mechanical planter can set eight to

ten thousand trees in an eight-hour day. The same two
men, planting by hand, under similar site conditions would
probably plant a total of no more than fifteen hundred in a
day. Moreover, using a planting machine usually eliminates the need for any elaborate site preparation. The
machine prepares the ground for planting as it goes along
(*Fig. 29*).

Figure 29. The planting machine breaks the sod and throws it to
the sides, thereby minimizing grass competition, at least for a year
or two. (*U. S. Forest Service*)

Needless to say, most commercial Christmas-tree growers who produce thousands of trees each year do all their
planting by machine. So if you plan to make a serious
business venture of growing Christmas trees, and if you
have enough of the right kind of land to warrant it, you will
want to consider seriously the advantages of acquiring a
planting machine.

How much land is *enough* for machine planting? It

would be hard to give a definite answer to this question that would apply to all localities, sites, and situations. If you have less than a total of forty or fifty acres, you would probably do just as well to stick to hand planting. On the other hand, if because of age, health, or disposition you do not relish the idea of planting two to three thousand trees by hand each year, you might want to invest in a tree planter for a smaller area.

What is the right kind of land? This question is easier to answer. In fact, it has been answered in part earlier in this chapter. Since the planting machine is pulled by a tractor, the land must be level enough for an ordinary farm tractor to maneuver on easily. The ground must be free from rocks, old tree stumps and roots, and heavy brush. Obstructions such as these interfere with the proper operation of the machine.

Planting machines cost several hundred dollars to buy and—you need a tractor to pull one. If you are a farmer and already have a tractor, you are all set. But for anyone starting from scratch, the cost of a tractor will boost his investment in machinery way up. Upon first thought, many beginning growers reject the idea of such an investment for a machine that may be used only a few days each year. On fairly large Christmas-tree farms, however, the tractor itself can be used throughout the year for pulling mowers and sprayers, for hauling harvested trees to the roadside, and so on. Some growers help offset the cost of their machinery by renting it out to other growers. You might even start a profitable little sideline business by contracting to do planting for other growers. In this way, your machine could pay for itself in a few years. On the other hand, there may be someone in your locality who already owns a planting machine that you can rent. In this way you can enjoy the advantages of machine planting without being burdened with the capital investment.

More and more Christmas-tree growers, nurserymen, and

interested firms throughout the country are providing planting machines and planting services for hire. They can
nearly always do the work for less than you could get it
done by hand, provided of course that your land is suitable
for machine planting.

There are several different makes and models of planting
machines on the market, but they all work on the same
principle. The typical planter is a small trailerlike affair
consisting of a rolling coulter (or circular knife blade) at the
front, a small double plowlike unit close behind, a tray or

Figure 30. Close-up of a machine planter (in raised position). The
rolling coulter (A) cuts the surface layer, the double plow (B)
throws the sod and soil to both sides, and the slanted wheels (C)
compact the soil after the man inserts the tree into the trench.
(*Harry A. Lowther Co.*)

platform for holding the trees, and a seat for the operator.
The whole thing is supported by two rubber-tired wheels,
that are closely set and inclined like the front wheels on
some farm tractors (*Fig. 30*). In operation the coulter cuts a
continuous slit in the surface of the ground; the plow digs a

trench, lifting and spreading the surface layers of vegetation and soil; the operator inserts the trees into this trench at regular intervals; and the wheels close the trench and compress the soil. As you can see, the machine does not actually plant the trees; it merely opens and closes the trench while the operator inserts the trees into the ground by hand.

Although the planting machine does not generally do as good a job of planting as can be done by hand, there is no real evidence that the mortality for machine-planted trees is much greater than for hand-planted. In fact, there are times when machine planting is superior to hand planting, especially if the hand planters are unskilled or careless. Moreover, any decrease in survival that might result from the use of a planting machine would doubtless be more than compensated by the greater economy of planting.

Anyone interested in planting by machine should certainly acquaint himself with all the various kinds available. Some are better adapted to flat land, some to hillsides, and others to light or heavy soils. The prospective buyer will, of course, want to consider these and other features as well as price before finally making his selection.

12

KEEPING PLANTATIONS CLEAN

When your planting is done, it would be nice if you could just heave a sigh, find yourself a shady spot to sit, and watch your trees grow into money. But this is not the way good Christmas trees are produced. Almost as soon as you have put your planting tools away, the job of maintenance begins.

First on the list of maintenance jobs is keeping the plantation clean. In order to assure good survival, growth, and development of the trees, the plantation must be kept free from natural vegetation that would overtop and shade out the young trees. Shading by competing vegetation probably results in more cull and deformed trees than any other cause.

During the first two or three years, the foremost task is to prevent a dense ground cover of grasses and herbaceous plants from developing. Such a cover can literally starve your trees to death, or at least drastically retard their growth. Later, after you have nursed the trees through this first ordeal, you are likely to have to cope with larger, woody plants—brush and trees.

The best way to avoid, or at least to minimize, the battle of the weeds, is to select a site that is comparatively free from such vegetation in the first place. Recently cutover forest land and long-abandoned, brushy fields are the most susceptible to rank weed growth, especially of the woody variety. Such sites should be rejected for Christmas-tree planting unless no other suitable land is available. Sites least likely to present a serious weed problem are old pasture land and recently cultivated fields. Here troublesome vegetation has been repeatedly killed, trampled, or plowed under for so many years that the seeds, roots, and sprouts have nearly all been eliminated. On such land, grasses and herbaceous plants may still flourish, but appropriate treatment each year will control them as well as the larger, woody plants.

You will probably have to settle for something less than the ideal site, however, so do not hesitate to accept a tract that has some scattered clumps of brush and a few unwanted trees. These can be eliminated without too much trouble before you plant.

CULTIVATION

Sooner or later, most beginning growers ask, "Should I cultivate my trees after they are planted?" By *cultivating* we mean plowing out or uprooting the weeds from between the rows of trees, much as corn and other row crops are cultivated. Some growers have this question answered for them, at least as far as machine cultivation is concerned. If their land is steep, rocky, or infested with old stumps and roots, machine cultivating is out of the question. Any such work they do will have to be done by hand. On land adaptable to the use of farm machinery, the question resolves itself to this: will it pay? This test, in fact, can be put to any job of maintenance that the grower contemplates. Unless you are reasonably certain that anything you do to maintain or improve your plantation is going to increase your ultimate income beyond the cost of doing it, the job is not worth doing.

To cultivate or not to cultivate, then, depends upon the value of the results to be attained. The purpose of cultivating is to reduce mortality, improve the form, and perhaps increase the growth rate of the planted trees during their first three or four years in the plantation, by removing all competing vegetation. These benefits are most sought after in plantations of slow-growing species, such as spruces and firs, that are intended for harvest when the trees are still small. Therefore, it is in such plantations that cultivation should perhaps be considered. As a general rule, however, cultivating is not worth the expense and is rarely practiced by experienced growers.

However, if you do plan to cultivate, your land should be plowed before planting, preferably the previous fall, unless it has been cultivated very recently for some other crop. Heavy sod or litter should be plowed under at least a year in advance of planting to allow time for the organic matter to decay and the soil to settle. This is to safeguard against root-drying air pockets in the soil in regions where droughts occur.

Most Christmas tree growers find it easier and cheaper to control grass, herbaceous plants, and small woody plants by mowing, applying herbicides, or, better yet, a combination of both. Indeed, a common method is to spray herbicide over rows, along both sides of a row of trees, or around individual trees and mow the untreated vegetation between the rows. This frees the young trees from the interference of competing plants but leaves a swath of vegetation for erosion control.

MOWING

There are several kinds and sizes of mowers on the market and better ones are constantly being developed. The most popular is a rotary type (similar to rotary lawn mowers), available in either riding or walking models (Fig. 31). Care must be taken of course to avoid mowing the planted trees along with the weeds, especially during the first year or two. With the smaller machines, it usually takes two passes between each two rows of trees to cut the full width of the space. However, these small mowers are easy to maneuver and are well adapted to plantations that may have crooked rows or irregular spacing between trees.

Figure 31. A power mower, even a "walking" model like this one, can save the Christmas-tree grower a lot of time and labor.

For large plantations a double mower pulled by a tractor and driven from the tractor's power take-off is commonly used. The tractor and mower straddle a row of trees and the two rotary knives (or sickles) cut to about the middle of the adjacent centers (spaces between rows). Such a rig more than doubles the amount of mowing that can be done within a given length of time. In order to use this machine safely and effectively, however, the alignment and spacing of your trees must be just about perfect. The big disadvantage of these larger, tractor-drawn mowers is that their use is limited to plantations where the trees are small enough to clear the underside of the tractor and the mower. Trees taller than three feet rub on the under parts of the tractor and on the arch of the mower, and the terminal buds or the bark or both are thereby damaged. However, mowing is most important during the first two or three years' growth, because it is during the early stages of tree development that grass and herbaceous plants are of greatest threat to the trees. So, in spite of their low clearance (a limitation which some manufacturers have tried to alleviate), this type of mower is one of the best labor-saving developments to date for the Christmas-tree industry.

HERBICIDES

Christmas trees can be successfully grown without herbicides, but avoiding their use will increase the time needed to produce a salable crop—perhaps by several years. At current tree prices, then, herbicides pay for themselves. So, subject to local conditions and laws, most experienced growers use herbicides to supplement or supplant mowing.

Commonly used chemicals are selective, killing only certain kinds of plants, so the chemical you choose will depend on the type of vegetation that is threatening your trees. Herbicides can be applied with a tractor-drawn machine that sprays a swath along both sides of a row of trees or with a portable sprayer that can be used to spray a small area around individual trees (*Fig. 33*).

Precautions

The use of herbicides is common practice today in agriculture and forestry to eliminate unwanted vegetation. Even homeowners use them to keep weeds out of their lawns. However, like all toxic substances, they must be used with great care and skill so as to prevent injury to other plants and animals. In fact, because of the potential hazard, herbicide use is strictly regulated by both federal and state law.

The federal government, through the Environmental Protection Agency (EPA), has set standards for pesticide use and handling. These regulations apply to insecticides, rodenticides, and fungicides as well as herbicides. Each state also has its own laws and regulations, some of which

Figure 32. Modern backpack sprayers are light, easy to use, and ideally suited for the small to medium-size operation. *(Solo Incorporated)*

are more restrictive than the federal ones.

By law, pesticides (including herbicides) must be registered with the EPA by the manufacturer. Each new chemical is classified into one of two categories: general use or restricted use. *General use* products are considered safe for use by the public as long as the instructions and precautions printed on the container are strictly followed. *Restricted use* pesticides can be applied only by a state-certified applicator, or under his direct supervision. Generally, the regulations governing the use of herbicides are less restrictive than those that apply to insecticides and rodenticides because the herbicides are less likely to be hazardous to animals or humans. As already mentioned, herbicides play an integral, indeed essential, role in modern agriculture. Nevertheless, the Christmas-tree grower must be familiar with the proper handling and potential hazards of any chemical he plans to use, as well as the laws and regulations that control its use.

Selection

Many different herbicides are available to the Christmas tree grower. Their selection and use are determined by the type of vegetation to be controlled, the species of trees being grown, and the time or season of application.

The herbicides commonly used in Christmas tree plantations can be divided into two types: preemergence and postemergence. Simply put, preemergence herbicides kill weeds before they start to grow in the spring, attacking seeds, buds, and roots; postemergence types kill growing plants. Some postemergence herbicides affect only those plant parts treated and are thus called "contact" types (e.g. Paraquat). These usually act within hours of application and so are not greatly affected by rain soon after treatment. Other postemergence herbicides, called "systemics" (e.g. Roundup), are absorbed into the plants through the leaves or stems and transported to the roots. These may take days or weeks to show any effects. Generally, contact types are best for annual weeds and shallow-rooted perennials, whereas systemics work best for deep-rooted perennial herbaceous plants as well as grasses and woody plants.

As mentioned earlier (chapter 6), one of the most versatile herbicides for Christmas-tree use is glyphosate (Roundup). When applied in a proper and timely manner, glyphosate will kill most annual and perennial weeds and grasses and many woody plants. However, because it has no effect on germinating weed seeds, glyphosate should generally be used in conjunction with a preemergence herbicide.

An effective way to control nearly all the weeds in your plantation would be to apply glyphosate in the fall (mid-to-late September) and schedule a preemergence treatment, such as atrazine (Aatrex), simazine (Princep), or oryzalin (Surflan), for the following spring. Dosages and exact time of application will depend to some extent on the species of Christmas trees growing in the plantation to be treated.

As good as Roundup is, some precautions must be observed in its use. If applied to the Christmas trees themselves while they are still growing, it can damage the foliage. The pines and Douglas-fir are more susceptible to such damage than the spruces and true firs. Also, newly planted seedlings are more likely to be injured than those that have been in the field a year or two.

To put this information in practical terms, here are some rules-of-thumb to guide you in planning Roundup treatments:

1. Delay applying Roundup at least one year after planting seedlings. If you did a good job of site preparation (see chapter 6) and applied a preemergence herbicide or mowed after planting, this will cause no problem.

2. Delay applying Roundup in the fall until your trees have "hardened off" (stopped growing). One clue to this is the condition of the terminal (topmost) bud: if it appears to be soft and succulent, the tree is still growing and it is too soon to apply Roundup.

3. Use a lighter dosage for pines and Douglas-fir than for spruces and the true firs.

4. Avoid spraying the leaders—especially those of the pines and Douglas-fir—with Roundup. This part is particularly susceptible to injury.

Although glyphosate is probably the best herbicide currently on the market for Christmas tree plantations, many others are available. Each one is registered for use *against* certain kinds of vegetation and *for* specific Christmas tree species. This information appears on the container label. So

your own local situation—site, climate, weed and tree species—should be considered when selecting herbicides.

Preparation

Herbicides can be applied either as dry granules or as
liquid sprays. The advantages of granules are that they can
be applied directly from the container they come in without
mixing; they can be applied by hand or with a common
lawn spreader; and their application can be more precisely
controlled on windy days. Nevertheless, spraying herbicides in liquid form is preferred by most growers because it
is cheaper, easier, and more versatile (two or more chemicals can be mixed together in a single application). Spraying can be done with either tractor-mounted or backpack
equipment. Tractor-mounted sprayers are much faster, of
course, but expensive and thus best suited for large plantations. Backpack sprayers are more practical and economi-
cal for small-to-medium-sized plantations (Fig. 32). An experienced worker can easily treat an acre per hour with
such equipment.

Herbicides to be applied as liquid sprays are usually dissolved or suspended in water. Mixing instructions (i.e. relative amounts of herbicide and water to use) are shown on
the container label. For mixtures especially appropriate
to your local conditions, consult your County Extension
Agent.

The strength or concentration of the herbicide is also re-
corded on the container and is expressed in *pounds* of active ingredient for liquid types and in *percent* of active
ingredient for dry granules. Prescribed rates of herbicide
application for various purposes are also expressed in these
terms, so it is a simple matter to calculate the amount of
herbicide needed for your particular job. For spot spraying
small areas, a given amount of herbicide is diluted in a gallon of water. However, for treating large areas, the volume
of water to be applied is determined first by calibrating the

sprayer (measuring its discharge rate per acre). Then the required amount of herbicide is determined by dividing the total desired amount of active ingredient by the number of pounds of active ingredient in each gallon of herbicide. Finally, that amount of herbicide is dissolved in the pre-determined volume of water.

These herbicides are toxic to most broad-leafed species—especially garden crops and other herbaceous plants—and therefore extreme care should be taken to prevent the spray solution from drifting over other trees and plants you do not want to kill. Even though Christmas-tree species are not permanently damaged by most herbicides, their needles do sometimes turn yellow or brown temporarily when exposed to these chemicals. So it is a good idea to concentrate your spraying on the weeds and keep the herbicide away from your trees as much as possible.

Application

For most weed species—grasses, herbaceous plants, and low brush—spray the herbicide directly onto the foliage. In some situations, depending on the species of trees you are growing, the kind of herbicide you are using, and the season, spraying may be done in swaths over the rows of trees. This is especially convenient if you are using tractor-drawn equipment with boom-type sprayers. However, as mentioned above, Christmas trees are variously susceptible to damage from herbicides. So, avoid spraying chemicals directly on the foliage of your trees unless the label specifically allows such application.

With backpack equipment, you can easily direct the spray under or around the trees, minimizing their exposure to the chemical. This can be done either in bands along the rows of trees or in circular spots around individual trees. If necessary, the remaining vegetation between the rows can be mowed. In extreme cases, when newly established plantations *must* be treated, you can protect the seedlings by covering them with plastic cones while spraying.

When using a back pressure sprayer, keep the pressure between thirty-five and forty-five pounds per square inch. Adjust the spray stream at the nozzle so that the spray angle is about forty degrees. Such a narrow spray concentrates the solution and prevents waste.

Trees taller than six feet but less than four inches in diameter should have the herbicide applied to the base of the trunk. This can be done any time during the year except during freezing temperatures. The only equipment needed is a back sprayer with a nozzle that can be adjusted for a very narrow stream. To conserve the spray material, the stream should never be wider than the tree's diameter. Wet the entire lower twelve to eighteen inches of the tree trunk all around, until the solution is running into the ground. This excess is not wasted because some of it penetrates the upper roots and hastens the kill.

Trees larger than four inches in diameter should be cut or girdled before the herbicide is applied. This kind of treatment, of course, requires an ax or saw in addition to the sprayer, and is most efficiently done with two people. One person either chops the tree down or hacks a frill around the stem as close to the ground as possible so that the inner bark is completely severed. The other sprays the herbicide on the cut surface of the stump or into and around the frill (*Fig. 33*). In either case, the exposed surface should be thoroughly wetted with the chemical.

One final precaution: once you have used a sprayer for herbicides, do not use it for anything else. It is almost impossible to remove every trace of these chemicals from the sprayer parts and the least amount left will cause damage if the sprayer is used for spraying insecticides in your garden.

Properly used, herbicides are a safe and efficient tool for the Christmas-tree grower; carelessly used, they can do more harm than good. So, before using any of these potent chemicals, familiarize yourself with the state laws and regulations governing its use; learn as much about herbicides in general, and the one you're considering in particular, as

Figure 33. Large trees should be frilled with an ax (arrow) before herbicide is applied.

you can (some good references are listed in the back of this book); and seek the advice and help of local experts.

ANOTHER OPTION

Some Christmas-tree producers control weeds by growing a crop of grain, grass, clover, or a mixture of these after each rotation of trees. This means that every six to ten years the land is completely cleared and the stumps removed or chopped into the soil with a heavy disk or rotovator, thereby eliminating any weeds that accumulated during the previous rotation. Troublesome perennials may be treated with herbicides. Such a procedure can be followed only on agricultural land and if you clearcut your plantation at the end of the rotation. After the grain is harvested, the area is kept mowed during the rest of the growing season. Trees are planted again the following spring, and mowing is done between the rows in the new plantation until the trees are so large that the mower cannot get between them. On land where this system can be practiced, it is a very effective way to prevent a heavy mat of sod and weeds from becoming permanently established. Although it minimizes the amount of weed control needed later on, it does not entirely eliminate the need for such work. In spite of this, and in spite of the fact that an extra growing season is needed between rotations, many growers feel that this practice pays high dividends in terms of tree quality.

13

SHEARING

Shearing is one of the keys to producing high quality Christmas trees. It results in the most important distinction between cultivated and wild trees. In simple terms, shearing is the trimming of the top and limbs of a tree to control its shape and the density of its foliage (*Fig. 34*). Not to be confused with pruning, which removes entire branches, shearing involves cutting only part of the current year's growth from the ends of the branches. The term came into use because early growers used an ordinary pair of hedge shears to do the job. *Shaping* may be a more descriptive word.

Judicious shearing of the trees will develop uniform spacing between branches, a symmetrical shape, and dense foliage: i.e., consistently high-quality trees. And *quality* is the one big aim of the Christmas-tree grower. Naturally you want to produce *good* trees—trees that will command the highest prices on the market. Experience has shown that most buyers will gladly pay premium prices for well-shaped, fully developed trees. It is no exaggeration to say that you will always be able to sell *all* the high-quality Christmas trees you can produce. So it will certainly pay to do everything possible to improve the quality of the trees. Learning and practicing the art of shearing is one of the surest ways to get good trees.

Once you know how to do it, shearing is a rather simple operation that can be done quickly. But done carelessly or in ignorance, it can do more harm than good. So, in order better to understand the principles involved, let us consider

Figure 34. A well-sheared Scotch pine. (*University of Minnesota, Agricultural Extension Service*)

first just what happens in the life process of a tree when it is sheared.

When you cut off the tip of the main stem, growth on that part stops abruptly for that year. In a week or ten days a cluster of new buds forms below the cut, and the following year these buds begin to grow. One of them develops into a new stem tip that grows straight upward and the rest develop into lateral branches, forming a new whorl. A similar process takes place when side branches are sheared.

Shearing then accomplishes three things. First, it allows

Figure 35(a). Spruce has visible buds all along its terminal stem.

you to shape the trees to suit the market: broad and rounded or narrow and columnar as local taste dictates. Next, it results in more branching and hence fuller, thicker foliage. But perhaps most important of all, it makes it possible to regulate the distance between the whorls or groups of branches on the main stem. In other words, by careful shearing, a tree can be forced to produce a new whorl of branches wherever wanted. This means that regardless of the variations in growth rate that may occur from year to

Figure 35(b). Pine has no visible buds on its terminal stem.

year, you can be sure of having proper and uniform spacing between the whorls and hence a tree that is pleasing to the eye. A fast or irregularly growing tree that has not been sheared has a wild, untidy look that most people shun in a Christmas tree.

WHEN TO SHEAR

The spruces and firs can be sheared at any time during

119

the year, but the pines can be sheared safely only during the height of the growing season. This is because the bud clusters form in different ways on trees in these two species groups.

The spruces and firs produce visible auxiliary buds along the stems and branches as the trees grow. These buds are fully developed and form clusters whenever the stem or branch immediately above them is removed. Pines, on the other hand, have no visible buds between the whorls (*Fig. 35*). The buds are there, to be sure, but they are dormant and hidden beneath the outer layer of bark. These buds, too, will develop and form clusters when the stem or branch above them is cut off, but the difference is that they will do so only during the active growing season. Except for a few of the southern pines, none of the species will grow any more that year after they are sheared.

What are the consequences of shearing pines out of season? Usually buds will fail to develop around the tip of the newly cut stem and the stem will die back to the last whorl. Thus a whole year's growth is lost and the presence of the dead tip will cause the next year's growth to be crooked. This is one reason why some shearing can do more harm than good.

The pines, then, should be sheared in late spring or early summer. The exact time depends more upon the stage of the new growth than upon the date, because the growing season varies according to the section of the country. A good guide to the best time for shearing pines is to begin when the new needles are about half the length of the old ones. Then you can usually count on a period of about two weeks for safe shearing.

The firs and spruces, as we have said, can be sheared at any time during the year. Most growers prefer to shear them during the dormant season, any time between late summer and early spring, before the new growth starts. Then the job can be done leisurely and need not interfere with other, more seasonal work.

METHODS OF SHEARING

Various tools may be used in shearing, the most common of which are hand clippers, hedge shears, power trimmers, and shearing knives. Each has its advantages and disadvantages. Hand clippers are precise and handy for getting into difficult places, but they make for slow work. Hedge shears are faster and easier to use, but somewhat tiring, although fatigue can be reduced if the shears have a rubber or plastic

Figure 36. Youthful crew using shears to shape pines. (*National Christmas Tree Association*)

bumper (Fig. 36). Shearing knives (specially designed with straight blades twelve to sixteen inches long) are the fastest hand tool for the job and for that reason are becoming the most widely used. They are easy to use, but hazardous, requiring metal or plastic leg, knee, and thigh guards for maximum safety (Fig. 37). Several types of power trimmers have been introduced in recent years and their use is increasing (Fig. 38).

Because the pines grow faster and are naturally less symmetrical, they need shearing and benefit from it much

Figure 37. This knife shearer wisely wears leg guards. (*Oregon State University, Extension Service*)

more than the spruces and firs. The latter, because of their slower, more uniform growth and their naturally conical shape, usually need (in addition to annual control of terminal stem length) no more than one or two light shearings to smooth out any rough spots. Density of foliage is rarely a problem because slow growth results in dense foliage. The pines, on the other hand, because of their irregular growth and shape, need three or four shearings in order to develop that trim Christmas-tree look.

You should begin shearing pines when they are about two feet tall and then shear them every year for about four years. The most convenient way to shear a small tree is to stand over it and work from above. In this way you can shear the whole tree without changing position. As the trees get larger, however, you will have to shear from the side and move around the tree.

For the first shearing, cut all the side branches necessary to give the tree the desired symmetry and shape. Unless the stem terminal is longer than twelve inches, do not cut it this first time. And at no time, either on the stem or on the branches, should you shear off more than the current year's growth. New growth is easily distinguished by the smaller size and lighter color of the needles.

The second and third shearings are concentrated on the terminal stem and the first (or top) whorl of branches. Cut the stem back to the same length as the distance between the last two whorls and the branches to about half this length. Do not cut any of the branches on the lower or bottom whorl unless they extend noticeably beyond the general crown outline. Ideally, a properly sheared spruce or fir should be in the shape of a cone. All the branches on each whorl should be the same length, and none of the branches should extend much beyond a line running from the top of the stem terminal to the tip of the lowest branch. Pines, on the other hand, should have a more rounded shape, especially at the bottom (*Fig. 39*). Although growth following shearing usually covers the scars of cutting, the last shearing should be the lightest of all, only heavy enough to do any necessary final shaping.

Because the numerous dormant buds on the pines are capable of developing clusters anywhere along the stem or branch, no special care is required in selecting the exact point at which to cut. Spruces and firs, however, should be cut just above one of the visible buds. Cutting an inch or more above a bud will leave a dead stub which will get in the way of the next year's growth and so deform it.

Long-needled pines, such as red and Austrian, should be sheared with a small pair of hand clippers or a shearing knife, rather than with hedge shears or power trimmers. The

Figure 38. Newly developed power trimmers promise to speed up the shearing process. *(Zum Zum Products, Inc.)*

reason for this can readily be seen in *Fig. 40.* The shears and power trimmers cut the adjacent needles off in a straight line, giving the trees a ragged appearance. These cut needles will never grow to normal length. By using the hand clippers or a knife, you can cut the stems without cutting the needles.

And now a word or two about how much to shear, or more specifically, how short to cut the terminal stem—for the length of the terminal stem determines to a large extent how much will be sheared off the lateral branches. Twelve inches is a good average length to leave the stem terminal, but this can vary according to current market trends and species. If trees are scarce in your area and anything green can be marketed, you can afford to leave the stem terminals longer and hence reduce your rotation by a year or two. On the other hand, if the buyers in your locality are more fas-

124

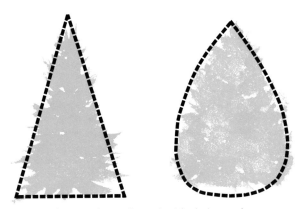

Figure 39. These outlines show the ideal shapes for spruces and firs (left) and pines (right).

tidious and demand denser trees, you may have to cut your terminals back to ten or even eight inches and delay harvesting for two or three years. The higher prices that such dense trees bring, however, will usually more than compensate for the longer rotation necessary.

The longer-needled pines, such as red, Austrian, and the southern pines, naturally look more bushy because of their long needles. The terminal stems on these species may be left somewhat longer without sacrificing the dense appearance of the tree.

With a little practice and experience, you can soon learn to shear sixty or more trees in an hour. If you figure your time at five dollars per hour, this means it will cost you six to eight cents every time you shear a tree. So for twenty-four to thirty-two cents per tree, you can shear four times during a rotation. This investment will greatly increase the value of your salable trees, and will also render many trees salable that otherwise you could not give away. No grower can afford *not* to shear his trees.

Figure 40. The natural appearance of the left branch of this red pine is the result of shearing with hand clippers; the right branch was cut with hedge shears.

BASAL PRUNING

Another recommended practice, closely associated with shearing is called *basal pruning*. This is the removal of all branches on a tree below the first good whorl eight to twelve inches from the ground (*Fig. 48*). Such pruning benefits the tree in several ways: (1) it eliminates energy-consuming foliage that must be removed anyway before a tree can be used, (2) it creates a "handle" on the tree for easy carrying and setting up, and (3) it minimizes the potential injury from certain insects and diseases (more about this in the next chapter).

Basal pruning should be done during the dormant season when the trees are at least three feet tall and preferably at the time of the first or second shearing. The job is best done with pruning shears, but if the branches are too big a pruning saw may be used.

Select a bottom whorl that has at least four strong, evenly spaced branches and prune off all branches below it. Be sure to prune close to the trunk so that the handle will be smooth and knot free when the tree is harvested.

14

PROTECTING THE PLANTATION

Every living thing has its enemies—and Christmas trees are no exception. One of the main jobs during the several years between planting and harvesting is to protect the trees from their enemies. This is the stage where most inexperienced growers fail. They delude themselves into thinking that once the trees are planted they will take care of themselves. We saw in a previous chapter that the grower has a big job to keep his trees free from competing vegetation. This chapter deals with the even bigger job of protecting the trees from their four major enemies: fire, animals, insects, and diseases.

FIRE

There is no need to dwell at length on the danger of fire to trees, especially to evergreen trees. The drastic results of forest fires have been dramatically publicized during the past half century. We need only add that in a solidly planted block of Christmas trees, fire usually means only one thing: swift and complete destruction of all the trees. A wildfire can destroy in minutes an investment that has taken several years to build up.

Although most fires occur in the dry seasons—late summer and early fall—evergreen trees are susceptible to burning at any time because they contain so much resin. So the grower must be on guard against fire, at least from early spring to late fall. The winter months are fairly safe because the cold and moisture make it difficult for fires to start.

The best way to fight fire is to prevent it. Never smoke, start a campfire, or burn brush in or near your plantation during the fire season. If you live at some distance from your plantation, try to make arrangements with a neighboring farmer or other resident landowner to be on the alert for fires or trespassers who might start fires. Get acquainted with your local, state, or federal fire warden; let him know where your plantation is; and give him all the cooperation you can in preventing and suppressing fires.

The next best thing to preventing fires is to keep them from spreading if they do start. In a Christmas-tree plantation this can be done by laying out a system of firebreaks around and throughout the plantation. A *firebreak* is a strip of ground ten to twelve feet wide that is kept free of all vegetation. A well-planned and well-kept network of firebreaks will usually confine a fire to the block of trees in which it starts. Most growers kill two birds with one stone by maintaining their firebreaks as roads. This not only gives them protection from spreading fires but also gives them ready access to all parts of the plantation, thus facilitating all phases of the work. Firebreaks are made by plowing in the spring and are kept fallow either by constant use as roads or by occasional disking during the growing season.

ANIMALS

Livestock must be kept out of the plantation. Although most domesticated animals will not browse on evergreen foliage if there is abundant forage of grasses and legumes, they are likely to damage the trees in other ways. In the first place, if cattle are left to roam freely in a new plantation, they will trample many of the young trees to death. Moreover, frequent ranging of large animals over a patch of ground will compact the soil so that the pore space in the surface layer is greatly reduced, thus hindering the free flow of water and air into and through the soil. And finally, larger trees can be permanently deformed if cattle rub against them and break or bark their branches or main stems. Therefore, if livestock have access to your plantation, you will have to fence them out. An electric fence will do the trick, provided of course there is a source of power readily available.

Sometimes certain kinds of wildlife may damage individual trees. Deer may browse on the foliage (especially during long, severe winters) and rabbits and rodents may gnaw around the stems and girdle them. It is not practical to fence these intruders out. Yet, in some areas wild animals can present serious problems to Christmas tree growers. One of the only practical defenses against them is the use of commercial repellents—chemicals that have disagreeable tastes or odors. Sprinkled around and under the trees, these products are intended to discourage the animals without harming them.

INSECTS

The damage that insects can do to evergreen plantations is tremendous; and the very insidiousness of these destructive agents multiplies their danger. You can see a fire burning your trees or a cow trampling them, and you can see the results immediately. But unless you are constantly on the alert and know just what to look for, you may not even notice the destructive work of insects until it is too late.

Only a few insects cause trees to die, and then usually only after repeated attacks. Some insects, however, may so disfigure a tree temporarily that it becomes unsalable as a Christmas tree. So it is very important to detect incipient insect outbreaks early enough to control them before they spoil the appearance of the trees. If insect outbreaks are allowed to go unarrested, the trees may take several years to regain their normal appearance. Fortunately, however, most of these enemies of Christmas trees can be controlled, and extensive damage can be prevented if their presence is detected soon enough and if the proper action is taken.

There are a great many different insects that may at one time or another prey upon Christmas trees—too many even to try to learn them all. But that would not be necessary anyway, because for any particular locality and species the grower will probably have to cope with only a few of them. The trouble is, you never know exactly which ones they will be and when they will attack. So the grower must constantly be on the alert for danger signals. He should inspect the trees closely every week during the spring and summer for insect activity or damage.

"Fine," you say, "I'll do it—but what do I look for?"

Many insects are so small and inconspicuous or, in the adult stage, so swift of flight, that they are seldom seen at work. Others do their dirty work in seclusion, either beneath the litter or inside the tree itself, and so are hidden from the casual observer. Of course, if you see a colony of sawfly larvae clustered around a branch tip on one of your pines, it will be obvious that they are up to no good and something should be done about them. But for the most part you will have better success if you train yourself to be on the lookout primarily for insect damage instead of the insects themselves. A good detective always investigates the crime first and then seeks the culprit. So in the discussion of injurious insects that follows, we have tried to classify the various insects according to the kind of damage they do. We have purposely avoided trying to describe in detail the many individual species; to do so would require several books the size of this one. Our advice to the beginner is to learn to recognize the symptoms of insect activity, to associate the symptoms with the general kind of insect that causes them, and then to carry this information to the nearest expert who is competent to identify the insect and recommend treatment. As you become more experienced and have suffered through an insect outbreak or two, you will naturally become more familiar with the insects that are locally important and their control. When in doubt, however, always seek professional help. An ill-conceived

Figure 41. Sawfly larvae at work. (*U. S. Forest Service*)

and ill-timed control effort will net nothing but a false sense
of security.

Now let us consider the major kinds of insect damage
and some of the insects that cause them. Insect damage is
likely to show up in any one of three different forms: defoliation, deformation, or discoloration.

Figure 42. After their work is done! (*U. S. Forest Service*)

Defoliation

First, you may notice that some of your trees are losing their needles, especially near the ends of the branches where the new growth is. This is usually caused by defoliating insects that consume the needles or at least cut them off. The most common of these insects are the sawflies, webworms, budworms, and bagworms. Some of these insects make their presence doubly conspicuous by spinning small bags that hang from the branches, or by webbing together twigs and cut needles into nests.

Sawflies. Sawflies are hairless caterpillars that often feed in colonies, usually beginning near the ends of the branches shortly after the growing season begins (*Fig. 41*). They devour entire needles, feeding mostly on the previous year's growth but sometimes on the new growth (*Fig. 42*). Although a tree can recover from moderate defoliation in a year or two, it is worthless as a Christmas tree until it does regain its needles. There are many different species of sawflies and at least one of them will attack most of the spruces, firs, and pines that are used for Christmas trees. Broods of these insects develop and attack quickly and are capable of causing much damage in two or three days.

Webworms. Webworms are so called because they spin webs around the needles that they feed upon. Sometimes these webs or nests become large globular masses of excrement with the larvae in silken tubes extending throughout the nest. Some of the more common species are: the pine webworm, which attacks red, white, jack, and pitch pines; the nesting sawflies, which feed on pines and other conifers; and the pine-tube moth, which attacks only white pine. The latter insect forms just a simple tube made of webbed needles.

Budworms. The young or larvae of budworms spend the winter in small webs formed under the bark scales. Early in the spring they emerge and bore into the opening buds, hence the name *budworms*. Later these larvae web together the tips of several twigs, forming rather conspicuous nests. Within these nests they cut off needles close to the bark, destroying much more foliage than they actually consume.

Bagworms. These insects are so named because each larvae forms a pear-shaped bag by webbing together particles of the foliage upon which it is feeding. Although known to feed on many of the species used for Christmas trees, bagworms are most injurious to the cedars.

Needle miners. Needle miners are minute insects that bore tunnels within needles during the larval state. Mined needles are usually found in groups, are yellow or brown in color, and appear to be hollow when held up to the light. They are commonly held together by webbing. Miners are particularly injurious to spruces.

Deformation

Another kind of injury results in dead or deformed shoots or branches. There are two general groups of insects that cause this damage by feeding on the buds and new shoots—borers and sap-sucking insects. The latter group also causes discoloration of the needles and so will be taken up under that heading. We shall confine our discussion in this section to the borers, which do most of their feeding within the twigs, shoots, and buds. Several species are known to attack Christmas trees, but there are three worst offenders.

Shoot moths. Eggs are laid usually in June and July on needles near the tips of twigs, where they soon hatch. The larvae bore into the base of needle bundles where they feed and remain until late summer when they bore into the buds. The following spring they bore into other buds and the new shoots, usually killing them and causing deformity of stems (*Fig. 43*). The European pine shoot moth is the most damaging species. It occurs throughout the Middle Atlantic states, westward to Illinois and Wisconsin, and in the provinces of British Columbia, Ontario, and Nova Scotia. Red, Scotch, and Austrian pines seem to be its favored foods, but other pines may be infested. Control is best obtained before an infestation becomes heavy.

Eastern pineshoot borer. Sometimes called the American pine shoot borer, the jack pine shoot borer, or the white pine tip moth, this insect attacks most species of pine

Figure 43. Damaged and deformed tips caused by the European
pine shoot moth. (*U. S. Forest Service*)

Figure 44. Eastern pine shoot borer caught tunneling through leader. (*U. S. Forest Service*)

grown for Christmas trees, as well as white spruce and Douglas fir. The larva bores into the new growth of the leader and the lateral branches in May and June, tunneling through the pith and emerging through an oval or circular hole, usually before any damage is noticed (*Fig. 44*). The readily detectable exit hole identifies this particular insect

Figure 45. The characteristic shepherd's crook shape of the leader on this pine is a clue to white pine weevil activity. (*U. S. Forest Service*)

species. Late in June, the injured shoots turn yellow and then reddish brown. Some lateral branches and many terminals fall over and break off several inches above the previous year's growth, leaving short, bare stubs. The ultimate result is deformed or crooked trees.

White pine weevil. This insect occurs over the entire range of eastern white pine. In addition to eastern white pine, it attacks Norway spruce (frequently and intensively), western white pine, jack pine, pitch pine, Scotch pine, and red spruce. It also attacks other pines and spruces, but less frequently and intensively. Eggs are laid in the spring in small bark punctures on the tree leader by the adult weevil. In a few days the eggs hatch, and the larvae feed on the inner bark as they burrow downward and around the leader, killing it. This causes the leader to wilt and bend over like a shepherd's crook (*Fig. 45*). Spraying is most effective if done in the early fall or early spring when the adults are feeding.

Zimmerman pine moth. This insect attacks most pine species but prefers Scotch pine. It bores into the base of shoots and branches, causing either forking or death of the shoot, depending on location. Telltale signs are "sawdust" caught in webbing near the base of branches along with abundant pitch. Branches may droop or even break off; branch ends may turn yellow or brown. Attacks on the bole may girdle the tree, so weakening it that it breaks off.

Galls. Galls are unsightly growths caused by insects on the new shoots of trees. These growths are common on spruce and may range from one-third of an inch to several inches long, depending on the insect species; they house the developmental stage of the insect. Two species are of most concern to the Christmas-tree grower. The eastern spruce gall aphid commonly attacks white and Norway spruce. Its galls are one-half to one inch at the base of the shoots, but may be extremely numerous on a tree (*Fig. 46*). The Cooley spruce gall aphid mainly attacks blue spruce.

Figure 46. Trademark of the eastern spruce gall aphid. (*U. S. Forest Service*)

The galls are one to three inches long and always appear on the end of the shoots. These attacks commonly kill the buds, thus deforming or weakening the tree. Douglas fir is also susceptible to this insect, but galls are not formed.

Discoloration

The third type of damage is discoloration; the needles of the trees turn yellow, brown, or red. This discoloration is often accompanied by a general loss of vigor. The insects that cause this damage are usually divided into two groups: the sap-sucking insects and the bark- and wood-boring insects. Although the outward symptoms for both are similar, their methods of attack are quite different. The sucking insects weaken the tree and cause discoloration of its foliage by feeding upon its nutrient juices. The borers, on the other hand, penetrate into the bark and wood, severing the network of tubes through which the upper parts of the tree receive water and mineral nutrients. Some of the sucking insects also attack buds and shoots, causing them to be deformed or forming galls on the branches. We will make no attempt to describe any of the sucking insects by individual species—there are too many of them. They are divided into four general groups: aphids, scales, spittlebugs, and red spiders.

Aphids. These soft-bodied, sap-sucking insects may be found feeding on the needles or bark of practically all species of Christmas trees. They usually feed in groups; some may be protected by masses of a white, cottonlike secretion. Damage caused may be in the form of discolored needles, deformed twigs (galls), or the death of entire branches.

Scales. Scale insects are so called because most enclose themselves in a hard, shell-like covering. They may be found on the needles, twigs, or stems. They feed by sucking the plant juices, which results in injury ranging from faded needles to the death of the entire tree. Several species of scale insects attack most of the common Christmas trees.

Spittlebugs. Spittlebugs are not known to do widespread damage to Christmas trees, although local epidemic attacks have been reported on red, Scotch, and white pines and Norway spruce. They damage the trees by sucking nutrients from the stems, thereby causing discoloration of the needles and retarding growth. The nymph of the spittlebug is clothed in a white, frothy mass that makes its presence conspicuous (*Fig. 47*). It may be easily controlled by spraying as soon as its presence is noted in the spring.

Red spiders. These are not true insects but mites—so small that the untrained observer seldom sees them. They cause damage similar to many of the sap-sucking insects. The damage usually appears as a general yellowing of the needles, sometimes accompanied by fine webbing. These pests will attack all Christmas-tree species. They can be controlled by any of a number of commercial miticides.

Figure 47. Foamy white material at base of needles signals a spittlebug infestation. (*U. S. Forest Service*)

Apply according to the manufacturer's label.

Pine root-collar weevil. This insect bores into the living part of the wood around the root collar of jack, red, Scotch, and Austrian pines. It may completely girdle the tree, causing it to lose color and eventually to die. You can often detect its presence by the blackened and pitch-soaked ground around the base of infested trees.

Pales weevil. This weevil represents a dual threat to Christmas trees because both the larva and the adult cause damage. Moreover, it attacks most species of Christmas trees—pines, spruces, firs, Douglas-fir, and redcedar—although it prefers eastern white pine. Eggs are laid beneath the bark of recently cut stumps, making a Christmas-tree plantation an ideal place for breeding. The larvae usually feed on the bark of these stumps but may migrate to the roots of nearby living trees, causing "flagging" (discoloration) of the branches. The adults cause the most damage, however. They feed at night on bark, girdling small branches and causing the foliage from the point of attack outward to turn yellow or brown.

Bark beetles. These are usually secondary insects; that is, they will attack only weakened trees, such as those suffering from prolonged drought. There are many kinds of bark beetles, some of which attack species of spruces, firs, and pines. Others attack only species of pine or species of spruce. Although widespread damage by these insects is not common in Christmas-tree plantings, there have been reports of localized attacks. The beetles kill by tunneling passageways in the inner bark. Once trees are attacked, it is difficult to save them. But spreading of the infestation can be retarded by cutting and burning all affected trees. The best protection is to keep the trees vigorous and to remove all dead and dying trees from the plantation and burn them.

Insect Control

The days of trying to annihilate insect populations with sprays alone are gone. As discussed in an earlier chapter, the use of pesticides—especially insecticides—is strictly regulated in most states, and some chemicals have been banned from use entirely. Furthermore, research and experience have shown that eliminating an insect from a certain area is not only impossible, but would probably do more harm than good, even if it could be done. Each plant and animal has its place in nature, and removing one of them that is bothersome to man could well upset the balance of things and cause even worse problems. That is what ecology is all about. So the purpose of insect control in a Christmas-tree plantation is not to exterminate an insect but merely to reduce its numbers to an acceptable level—and this by whatever means is safe as well as effective.

More and more emphasis in "pest" control is being

placed on cultural or biological measures and less on chemicals. For example, insect infestations in a Christmas-tree plantation can often be minimized, if not prevented altogether, by keeping the trees healthy and vigorous. This means providing them with ample growing space, controlling competing vegetation, and fertilizing if necessary. Another way to reduce insect populations is to keep the plantation clean, again by eliminating brush, herbaceous, and grassy vegetation that serves as cover and breeding ground for the Christmas trees' insect enemies.

In addition to these general preventive measures, in some instances certain cultural practices can control specific insects. Here are two examples.

Larvae of the previously mentioned European pine shoot moth spend the winter in the buds at the ends of branches. However, only those in branches below the snowline will survive; those in buds not covered by snow will generally be killed by the subzero cold. To reduce the population of this insect, then, it is only necessary to prune off the lower whorl of branches whose tips would likely be buried in snow for extended periods during the winter (*Fig. 48*). In some cases, such pruning can delay harvest for a year, but, as mentioned in the previous chapter, these lower branches are usually pruned away to make a "handle" on the tree anyway.

Another insect on the Christmas tree grower's "most wanted" list is the pine root-collar weevil, also described earlier. The adult weevil must have a cool, dark, moist place to live, so it spends summer days beneath the litter and duff near the trunk of a pine tree. Pruning off the bottom branches and scraping or raking away all the organic matter down to the mineral soil for about a foot around the trunks of your pines will eliminate this bug's summer home and make life just about impossible for him.

Research is continuing to devise similar controls for other insects, so it will pay to keep in touch with new developments.

Figure 48. Buried branch tops of the pines in the foreground invite shoot moth attack. Basal pruned trees behind are relatively safe—and more easily cut, hauled, and set up. (*U. S. Forest Service*)

All this is not to say that insecticides are never used. When an insect infestation gets out of hand and no other control is feasible, the grower must resort to chemical sprays or suffer a crippling financial loss. But these should be used as a last resort.

Most insects that damage Christmas trees can be controlled by spraying. The trick is, however, to select the right insecticide and to apply it at the right time. This requires a technical expert who can determine the exact species of insect you are dealing with and is familiar with its life history and feeding habits. Armed with this information, as well as with a knowledge of the appropriate registered chemicals, he can then prescribe a treatment.

There are various kinds and sizes of spraying equipment that can be used for spraying Christmas-tree plantations. The most common type is the hydraulic sprayer, ranging in size from one-and-a-half-gallon knapsack sprayers to machines holding three to four hundred gallons and capable of pump pressures up to a thousand pounds per square inch. Another popular type is the mist blower, which also ranges from back-pack to truck size. The chief advantage of the mist blower is that it can handle highly concentrated sprays and hence requires less gallonage per acre. Extensive plantations may be sprayed by airplane. Numerous commercial companies have planes equipped to do this work. The type of equipment you should use depends among other things on the size of your area and its accessibility and the insect to be controlled.

Since there is no sure way to predict just when or where a serious insect outbreak may occur, your best protection is unceasing vigilance. So remember:

1. Inspect your plantation frequently, especially in the spring and early summer.
2. Be alert for
   a. Loss of needles.
   b. Bags, webs, or spittle in the trees.
   c. Brown or deformed shoots or buds.
   d. Discolored needles and loss of vigor.
   e. Unusual insect activity.
3. Unless you are sure what the cause is, call in an expert immediately. The earlier you catch an outbreak, the better are your chances of subduing it.

DISEASES

Christmas trees are susceptible to a variety of diseases. Like human diseases, some are killers, some are maimers, and some merely nuisances. Here again, early detection and control are essential and professional assistance is recommended. Frequent inspections of the plantation, weekly during spring and summer, will allow you to catch a disease in its early stages and make control easier. Inspections for both insects and disease can be made simultaneously.

Diseases tend to be rather specific; that is, each one attacks only certain species of trees. Diseases of pines, for example, are rarely found on any other conifer species.

Those that do attack other plant species during their life cycles (cedar-apple rust and white pine blister rust, for example) seem to select broad-leafed species rather than conifers for their "alternate hosts."

This selectivity is a boon to the grower: he has only to learn to identify those diseases that are likely to infect the particular tree species he is growing. Because of this, in the discussion that follows we group individual diseases according to the tree species they attack. This facilitates comparing symptoms between diseases rather than between tree species. There are too many diseases to consider all of them here, so we will concentrate on the most important—those that are most prevalent or do the most damage.

Pines

Ironically, the pines, which have become the most popular Christmas-tree species (at least in the eastern states) seem to be susceptible to the most diseases. And Scotch pine is hardest hit of all, partly because it is not native to North America, and introduced trees have not had time to develop any immunity to local diseases. Of course, the very prevalence of the pines works against them; the more widely a tree species is planted, the easier it is for disease to spread. On the bright side, however, plant disease researchers concentrate their efforts on the worst culprits, and so controls for them are usually developed first.

Lophodermium needlecast. This disease was not a serious problem in Christmas-tree plantations until about 1970 when widespread damage began to appear in the Lake states region, chiefly on Scotch pine but also on red. Since then it has become common throughout the northern, eastern, and northwestern parts of the United States, and southeastern and southwestern Canada. The first symptom is tiny brown spots with yellow margins on the needles in early spring (*Fig. 49*). This is followed by complete browning of the needles. These needles fall off later in the summer.

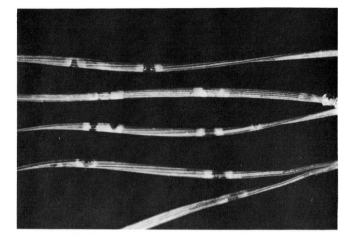

Figure 49. Yellow-bordered brown spots, clearly visible even in a black and white photo, are an early symptom of Lophodermium.
(*U. S. Forest Service*)

When more than 20 percent of the trees' foliage has turned brown by May or June, this is the signal to call a plant pathologist for positive identification. (Many disease symptoms are so similar that it takes professional laboratory examination to tell them apart.) Some fungus sprays (fungicides) are effective for controlling this disease and are registered for use in most states. The key to control is early detection, when the infection is light, and proper timing of the treatment. Spraying must be done in late summer or early fall, before the spores are released from the tiny black fruiting bodies that appear on the dead needles. If infection is serious, three treatments may be necessary, one each in July, August, and September.

Brown spot needlecast. This disease will infect several pine species, but is of most concern to the grower of Scotch pine in the north-central states, Minnesota south to Arkansas. Symptoms are similar to those of Lophodermium, except that the needles turn brown in the fall instead of in

Figure 50. Needles of brown spot infested trees turn brown in the fall and then fall off, beginning at the bottom of the tree. (*U. S. Forest Service*)

spring. Browning is most conspicuous in the lower half of the tree (*Fig. 50*). Again, positive identification can only be made in the laboratory. Unless the disease is checked, needles of all ages will become infected and fall off the tree. Light infection reduces or destroys a tree's value as a Christmas tree for at least a year or two; heavy infection may eventually kill it. The disease can be controlled with a fungicide applied about mid-June. In wet years, another spraying may be necessary a month later. Consult your local pesticide expert for advice and help on what chemical to use and how to use it.

Scleroderris canker. Another relative newcomer to the Christmas-tree scene, this disease kills small trees and the lower branches of larger ones (five to ten years old). Look for orange discoloration at the base of red and Scotch pine needles early in May. When infection has progressed further, scraping away the bark of dead branches will reveal a green discoloration. As yet there is no sure control for this disease, but its presence should be reported to your local authorities immediately upon detection because movement of infected trees is regulated by quarantines. Until an effective control is developed, it would be wise to plant other tree species in areas where Scleroderris is or may become prevalent.

Dothistroma needle blight. A widespread and severe disease of pines in the Southern Hemisphere, this disease was first reported in this country in 1940. Although many pines are susceptible, Austrian pine is its favored host; growers of other pines need not worry about this one. Symptoms are scattered spots, ranging in color from yellow to red, appearing on the needles in midsummer or fall. Some of these spots may develop into red bands that encircle the needles, hence the name "red band disease" is a common alias. The tip of the needle beyond the band turns brown and dies, while the lower part may remain green. Infected needles commonly fall off the next spring or sum-

Figure 51. Pruning off infested branches helps to halt spread of white pine blister rust. (*U. S. Forest Service*)

mer, so bare spots on the inner, older parts of a tree are also symptomatic. The disease can be controlled with the appropriate fungicide; usually only one application a year is necessary.

White pine blister rust. This fungus is confined to the white pines and is especially destructive to the eastern and western white pines. It is most common in the North, where summers are cool and humid. The first visible symptom is patches of dead foliage, red brown in color. Closer examination will reveal spindle-shaped cankers below the dead foliage and a yellowish discoloration of the bark around the edges of these cankers. The fungus progresses down the branches to the main stem, which it eventually girdles, killing the tree. As long as the disease is confined only to the branches, an infected Christmas tree may be saved. If there are no cankers on the trunk or within four inches of it, the fungus can be halted by pruning off the infected branches (*Fig. 51*). Once the infection reaches the main stem, however, the tree is doomed. The fungus must spend part of its life cycle on currant or gooseberry bushes, so the traditional method to combat this disease has been to destroy all such bushes within a radius of at least half a mile. This is hardly feasible for the typical Christmas-tree grower, however. If these alternate hosts are common in your area, it would be best not to plant any of the susceptible pines.

Blue Spruce

Rhizosphaera needlecast. Although this disease of blue spruce may kill some trees, it is chiefly known to cause discoloration and shedding of needles, rendering the trees useless for the Christmas-tree market. Infection occurs in May or June, but early symptoms do not appear until late fall or the following spring. Tiny, fuzzy, black dots appear on the needles (*Fig. 52*). The infected needles turn yellow in July and purplish brown in late August, after which they drop. Damage is most severe on the lower part of the tree. Chemical spraying will control the disease.

Douglas-Fir

Swiss needlecast. Found exclusively on Douglas-fir, this disease causes loss of needles, beginning with the oldest. Obvious symptoms do not occur until the second summer. Then needles become yellowish green, sometimes in a mottled pattern. At this time fuzzy black dots will appear in the needles, similar to the symptoms found with rhizosphaera needlecast on blue spruce. Later that year some of the needles may turn brown and drop. During the third year, the rest of the needles turn completely brown and fall, resulting in a thin-foliaged tree. Swiss needlecast can be controlled by a fungicide spray during early June and again in early July.

Rhabdocline needlecast. This disease is similar in many ways to Swiss needlecast, causing a mottling and premature shedding of two- and three-year-old needles. Both the coast and (especially) mountain varieties of Douglas-fir are attacked. Fungicide application when the new needles are about one inch long is a recommended control.

Figure 52. Rhizosphaera damage is most conspicuous on lower part of tree. (*U. S. Forest Service*)

Eastern Redcedar

Cedar-apple rust. This is another disease that must have two different hosts during its life cycle. It is common on eastern redcedar and some of its varieties wherever apple, crab apple, or hawthorn trees are growing. Symptoms on redcedar are galls that produce showy, orange-colored, gelatinous "horns" in the early spring. Later in the year, the galls become hard and brown and are conspicuous and unsightly on the trees, causing downgrading for Christmas-tree use. The best way to avoid this disease is to plant redcedar at least a mile from apple trees of any kind. If this is not possible, you can spray the trees early in the spring, although this latter treatment may cause objectionable browning of the needles. If there are only a few apple trees within a mile radius of your plantation, it might be easier to spray them instead.

Prevention and Control

Damage and loss from tree diseases can often be minimized, sometimes even avoided, if certain practical preventive measures are followed. Some of these have been mentioned before, others may seem self-evident, but combined they can go a long way toward keeping your plantation disease-free.

Locate your plantation site carefully. Avoid:
- Poor sites that will preclude vigorous growth of trees.
- Sites near natural or planted stands of trees of the species you plan to plant; these can serve as infection reservoirs for various diseases.
- Sites where alternate hosts of diseases common to the species you want to plant are prevalent.

Plant only healthy nursery stock. This may seem obvious,

but many plantations have been doomed to failure from the start because some of the seedlings planted were already infected with disease.

Keep your trees healthy. Plant carefully, control competing vegetation, remove potentially infectious debris, and fertilize if necessary.

Avoid damaging your trees. Careless use of tools and machinery can cause wounds that may serve as entries for disease organisms.

Do not leave live branches on stumps. These lower branches are especially susceptible to disease and can help perpetuate infection.

Do not shear when trees are wet. Moisture on shearing tools may carry infection from one tree to another. Sterilize tools after each use.

Plant disease-resistant varieties. Keep abreast of the newest varieties available, as reported in the current Christmas-tree literature.

Plant more than one species. This is especially advisable where disease is a serious problem. If a catastrophic outbreak of one disease does occur, your entire investment will not be wiped out.

Once more we are deliberately avoiding getting into the specifics of chemical control of diseases. Although fungicidal sprays are an effective, and sometimes the only, means of controlling many Christmas-tree diseases, their safe, proper, and legal use often calls for an expert in the field.

NONINFECTIOUS "DISEASES"

Sometimes what may look like a disease or an insect attack is not that at all, but rather the symptoms of damage caused by weather, water, chemicals, or even animals. The Christmas-tree grower should be familiar with such symptoms so as not to be fooled into thinking his trees are diseased or infested when, in fact, they may be suffering from such things as extremes in temperature or drought.

An untimely frost, in late spring or early fall, when the trees are still growing, can cause drooping and discoloration of tender new needles or buds.

Rapid temperature changes during the winter, often at sunset and sunrise, can cause a browning of needles called *winter burn,* especially on the south side of the trees (*Fig. 53*).

Figure 53. The entire plantation on the right has turned brown from winter burn; the more hardy variety of Scotch pine on the left escaped and remains a healthy green. (*U. S. Forest Service*)

A similar problem, *winter drying,* also causes needles to turn brown and sometimes droop. It occurs when warm, dry winds in late winter or early spring induce rapid transpiration from the needles while the ground and the lower parts of the trees are still frozen.

Drought causes wilting and discoloration of foliage, usually from the top down. Drought-weakened trees are readily susceptible to real diseases.

Improperly applied herbicides can cause yellowing or browning of needles and curling of new growth.

Trees growing near a road where salt is used to melt ice may turn brown if any of the salt is blown or thrown onto the foliage or onto the ground above the roots. Such discoloration is most pronounced on the side of the trees facing the roadway.

Air pollution can produce various disease symptoms, depending on the source.

Mice or other rodents, feeding on the bark at the base of a tree, can completely girdle it. This causes the entire tree to turn brown and eventually die. So, before you attribute the death of a tree to some disease, examine the stem near the groundline. If bare wood is exposed all around it, the tree has been the victim of a field mouse or one of his cousins. Where such damage is extensive, some strategic poisoning may be called for.

15

GRADING
CHRISTMAS TREES

Most agricultural and many manufactured products are sold by grade. Such varied commodities as meat, canned goods, and lumber are all assigned grades based upon quality, and are priced accordingly. As yet there is no standard, generally applied system for grading Christmas trees, although the basis for such a system exists in the *United States Standards for Grades of Christmas Trees*, established by the U.S. Department of Agriculture and revised in 1973. Some states have adopted these grades, or modifications of them, but so far most grading is done on a voluntary basis. In most markets today, trees are either salable or they are not, and that is about as far as it goes. As the industry grows and refines itself, however, some sort of grading is bound to come into general use. Perhaps by the time your first block of trees is ready to be harvested it may be common practice to grade trees in your locality.

PURPOSE OF GRADING

Grading any product has a twofold purpose: to protect the consumer and to encourage the producer. When a man buys a graded product, he knows that if he pays a premium price he will get premium quality. Similarly, when a man sells a graded product, he knows that premium quality will bring a premium price. As a result, the consumer learns to relate price and grade, and the producer is induced to concentrate on quality. Grading, then, tends to standardize prices and improve products. In other words, if a Christmas-tree grower can be sure that high-grade trees will bring correspondingly higher prices, he will probably make a greater effort to produce quality trees. Now, of course, the principle of higher prices for better products holds true whether or not the product is actually graded according to a fixed and rigid set of rules. It certainly holds true in the Christmas-tree industry. A buyer is usually willing to pay more for a tree that suits his taste exactly than for one that for some reason is less desirable. A practical, standardized grading system would benefit the industry by giving it more stability, by establishing common grounds for carrying on transactions, and by creating better understanding and confidence among producers, wholesalers, and retailers.

Before Christmas-tree grading can become an accepted, universal practice, certain obstacles must be overcome and some questions answered. For example, growers have found that unless grades are spelled out in detail, it is difficult for all concerned to agree upon them. Moreover, any set of grades will apply only in a general way to all species. If detailed grades are desired, they will have to be varied by species or at least by groups of species. Another difficulty is that if standardized grades are generally adopted, they are very likely to be made mandatory by law. Such a situation would work hardships on growers whose markets do not require grading. And finally, grading trees can be a time-consuming and costly process. None of these hurdles need be insurmountable, however; most of them will probably be eliminated or minimized when a suitable grading system is finally adopted.

BASIS FOR GRADES

When grading does become standard practice, how will it work? What will the system be based on? These questions are of some concern to the beginning grower because the way trees are graded may well influence the way he manages his plantation. Fortunately, the groundwork has been laid by various groups of growers and the essentials, at least, have been fairly well agreed upon. There is, or will be, nothing mysterious about Christmas-tree grades. They are based upon characteristics which we have mentioned over and over again throughout this book: form and density of crown, color and condition of needles. But let us just review these quality-determining characteristics from the standpoint of grading.

It is axiomatic that since the consumer is the final judge of quality, whatever he judges to be good or bad in a tree must be reflected in the grading system. What, then, does the consumer look for in a Christmas tree?

Above all, he wants his tree to look fresh, clean, and healthy. The needles should be pliable and firmly attached; the tree should be free of moss, lichens, and other debris; and it should have a natural look, typical of the species.

Form

In form, he looks for symmetry first, then the ratio of width to height, and finally general outline. Lopsided crowns or crooked stems he rejects immediately. However, choice in width-to-height ratio varies, usually according to species. Those who prefer the pines seem to go for shorter, wider trees and those who prefer the spruces and firs like their trees to be tall and slender. Preferences in outline or shape also seem to vary with species. Everyone insists upon a pointed top, but the pine enthusiasts look for rounded sides and an arrowhead shape, and the spruce and fir buyers want a straight, sharper taper and a wedge shape (see *Fig. 39*).

Density

The next thing the buyer looks for is density of the crown—in other words, the amount of light or open space that can be seen through the crown. This is determined by the number of branches in a whorl, the distance between whorls, the number of branchlets on each main branch, and the number and size of needles. Trees of medium density are usually preferred, provided the foliage is distributed uniformly. Excessively dense trees are not popular because they are too hard to decorate.

Color

Color of needles is also an important consideration in selecting a Christmas tree. Most buyers have some sort of color preference in trees. Some like light green needles, others dark green; some prefer a blue green shade and others a yellow green. Obviously, variations in shade cannot be used in grading trees because this is a matter of personal taste. But any departure from the normal green color for a particular species, such as needles that are distinctly yellow or brown, automatically lowers a tree's appeal and hence its market value. Such abnormalities in color may be caused by diseases, insects, drought, sudden drops in temperature, or nutritional deficiencies.

Condition

And finally, the general condition of the tree influences its grade. An otherwise high-quality tree can be seriously degraded if the foliage, limbs, or trunk are damaged in any way: staining or discoloration; gaps or "holes" in the foliage; broken, dead, or deformed branches; missing needles; etc. The buyer will have nothing to do with a tree that is in any way abnormal or that has obviously had rough treatment.

These are the things, then, that determine the grade of a tree. They all have one thing in common and that is that most Christmas-tree buyers feel the same way about them. Everyone likes a tree that has a pleasing, symmetrical shape, reasonably uniform density, and fresh healthy-looking foliage. Characteristics that the majority of buyers do not agree upon or that vary by species cannot be used in grading trees—for example, tree size, aroma, needle length, and needle retention.

The accompanying table outlines the *United States Standards for Grades of Christmas Trees,* previously mentioned. Our purpose in presenting this table is to summarize in an orderly way the general criteria and standards for grading Christmas trees that will inevitably be incorporated into any universally adopted system. Its chief value to the prospective grower is that it lists the features that go to make up a "good" Christmas tree. But it will also help to acquaint him with the current status of grading so that he can more readily keep abreast of future developments.

There is little doubt that Christmas-tree grading is on the way. How long it will be before a suitable system is adopted universally by the industry, no one knows right now. The beginning grower should be interested but not greatly concerned, because regardless of the grading system used, the best trees will always command the highest prices. And everyone's objective, of course, is to produce only the best.

United States Standards for Grades of Christmas Trees

Grade	General appearance	Density of foliage	Taper[a]	Damage
U.S. Pre-mium	Fresh	Medium or greater	Normal 40–90 per-cent	All four faces[b] free of damage
U.S. No. 1 or U.S. Choice	Clean	Medium or greater	Normal	Three faces free of damage
U.S. No. 2 or U.S. Stan-dard	Healthy Well-shaped Butt trimmed[c]	Light or greater	Normal Candlestick (less than 40 per-cent) Flaring (more than 90 per-cent)	Two adja-cent faces free of damage
Cull	← —————— Fails to meet any of above ——————→			

[a] Taper is the relation of a tree's width to its height, expressed in percent.
[b] A *face* is the surface of a tree visible from eight to ten feet and is considered to include one-fourth of the tree's circumference.
[c] Handle not less than six inches nor more than one and three quarters inches for each foot of height.

16

HARVESTING

The long-awaited day has finally come. You have mowed, sheared, protected, and generally mothered your trees for several years and now you are ready to begin harvesting. If it were not for the fact that you have some younger trees coming along, you would be almost reluctant to see this first batch go. Almost, that is, but not quite, because so far your business has been operating in the red. Your outlay in time, labor, and money has been gradually mounting throughout the rotation and your income has been nil. Naturally, you are getting anxious to begin making entries in the receipts column of your ledger.

Although you will not actually harvest the trees until late fall, you should begin making plans and preparations several months in advance, during the preceding summer. In this way, when harvesting time does come, you will be ready and able to get the job done quickly, efficiently, and economically. The first thing to decide is which trees to cut. This will depend upon your system of management and method of planting, as discussed in Chapter 9.

CLEARCUTTING

If you are using the block system of management and have been planting one block each year, the simplest way to harvest is to remove all the trees on the oldest block and replant again the following spring. The trouble with this procedure is that not all the trees will be ready for market at the end of the rotation. Some will be too small or poorly formed to make salable Christmas trees. So you must decide what to do with these rejects.

A few growers prefer to harvest all the salable trees in one year, destroy the rest, and start all over again the next year. They feel that although some trees are lost, in the long run this is the most efficient way to operate; it makes all their work easier from planting to harvesting. Others, reluctant to destroy any individuals that do not make the grade as Christmas trees, have developed lucrative sideline markets for these trees. (See Chapter 18.)

Still other growers get around the problem by spreading the harvest over a two- or three-year period so as to allow the slower growing trees to reach salable size and the less shapely ones to be sheared again. Then, after the second or third cut, they destroy or otherwise dispose of all the remaining trees and get ready to replant. This delays the next rotation, but those who follow the practice feel that it is better to see as many trees as possible through to a sale, even if it takes a couple of years longer, than to waste all the time and care that have been invested in them during the standard rotation period. On the other hand, those who prefer to cut all the trees on a block at once feel that they can make more money by starting a thousand new trees on an acre than by nursing along a hundred or so older ones. In this way, although they lose some of their investment on the first rotation, they get a couple of years head start on the second.

Whether you clearcut the block in one, two, or three years will depend in part upon the number of unsalable trees you have left after the first cut. If 20 percent or more of your trees are not ready to be marketed the first time, it will probably pay you to retain them in the plantation a year or two longer, provided, of course, that they are in good enough shape to develop into salable trees in that time. If just a few scattered individuals remain, however, the best thing to do is get rid of them in one way or another so that you can make a new planting in the spring. The number of trees that cannot be cut for Christmas trees can be held to a minimum by doing a good job of shearing throughout the rotation.

Your planting method may also influence your harvesting plans. If you do your planting by machine you will have to practice some sort of clearcutting, because in order to use a mechanical planter effectively the land must be completely bare of trees.

SELECTIVE CUTTING

Many of the small growers and some of the larger ones practice what is called *selective cutting*. They begin harvesting as soon as they have trees large enough to sell and they continue cutting the merchantable trees each year until the original planting has been completely removed. Each spring they replant the vacant spots left by the trees cut the previous fall. Such spot planting must, of course, be done by hand. This results in a plantation containing all ages and sizes of trees, a situation that has some disadvantages, as we have seen before. Some growers who practice selective cutting do not replant until all the original trees have been removed. This can take as long as six years and delays the start of the next rotation accordingly, but it is necessary if replanting is to be done by machine. Each grower must decide for himself which harvesting system is best suited to his operation.

TOOLS

Most commercial growers today use power saws for harvesting. Although rather expensive to buy, a power saw will pay for itself within a few years if your annual harvest runs to three thousand or more trees. A small, lightweight chain saw is perhaps the handiest tool for this purpose (Fig. 54). It is fast, very portable, and has other uses around the Christmas-tree plantation, notably brush removal. Also commonly used is a shoulder-mounted brush cutter, which eliminates crouching or bending when harvesting trees (Fig. 55).

If you would rather not buy or use a power saw, your best bet is probably a small bow saw. Although not as fast as the power tools, in the hands of a skilled cutter it produces a flat, square cut with a few quick strokes. You can also use a regular pruning saw with a four-to-six-foot handle, which enables you to reach under the trees without interference from the lower limbs.

Figure 54. The chainsaw is a favorite tool for harvesting Christmas trees. *(U.S. Forest Service)*

MARKING

In order to save time and misunderstanding during the actual cutting operation, you should select and mark the trees to be removed a month or so in advance of harvesting. This is especially important if you are going to cut only part of the trees that year. Tie or wire a conspicuous tag (red, yellow, or white) near the top of each tree that is to be cut.

Figure 55. Another popular harvesting tool is the power brush cutter, which has the advantage of allowing the operator to work in an upright position. *(U.S. Forest Service)*

Then when you or your helpers come through the plantation at harvest time, you will not need to waste time selecting or locating the trees destined for removal.

WHEN TO HARVEST

One of the advantages of plantation-grown Christmas trees is that they do not have to be harvested as early as those cut from remote wild land. The best time to harvest, however, depends in part upon the species. Cutting of spruces should be postponed as long as possible, preferably until just before time to deliver them to the customer. The reason for this is that spruces shed their needles faster than any other species upon drying and so should remain on the stump as long as possible. The firs retain their needles longer than the spruces, but it would probably be a good idea to schedule harvesting of these species for late in the season too.

If needle loss, especially on the spruces, is a serious problem in your area, you may want to consider applying an antidesiccant or needle-retention spray to these species in early fall before harvesting. Available from most Christmas-tree industry suppliers, these sprays can be applied with any mist blower (*Fig. 56*). They are clear and harmless and won't wash off or retard growth.

Pines may be cut as early as six weeks before delivery to the market and still hold their foliage firmly throughout a long holiday season. There are at least two advantages to such early cutting.

First, the weather and road conditions are likely to be more favorable in the fall than in early winter. In fact, you can afford to wait until conditions are favorable, whereas if you put off your cutting until late in the season, you will be under pressure and may have to work when the weather and roads are bad.

The second advantage of early cutting is that it often prevents yellowing of the needles in some species of pine. Certain strains of Scotch and jack pine sometimes suddenly turn yellow in early winter. What causes this untimely phenomenon is not exactly known, since it does not happen every year. Some growers feel that it has something to do with sudden drops in temperature. At any rate, it can be serious if it strikes an entire plantation, because many buyers, understandably, will refuse to accept shipment of

Figure 56. Backpack mistblower is handy for applying needle-retention or colorant sprays. (*U. S. Forest Service*)

trees in this condition. If the trees are cut early, however, before this yellowing occurs, and are properly stored, they will retain their natural color regardless of temperature changes.

If you should happen to postpone harvesting these species too long or if you have a yellowing problem anyway, you have two alternatives. You can keep the trees in the plantation for another year—they will "green up" again the following spring—and hope the yellowing does not recur the next fall. This requires no out-of-pocket expense, but it does delay your income from those trees for another year. And it is risky: you can't be sure the trees won't turn yellow again. Most growers now prefer the second alternative—applying colorant sprays in the fall before harvest. Like the needle-retention sprays previously mentioned, these can easily be applied with a mist-blower, are safe to use, and harmless to the trees. Although green in various shades is the most common color used, some growers kill two birds with one stone by covering some of their yellowed trees with pastel shades ranging from white to pink or blue, thereby taking advantage of a small but insistent market for "off-color" trees. These colorants have the added advantage of reducing moisture loss.

If you do cut your trees several weeks before they are due to be shipped, do not leave them lying on the ground in the plantation where they are exposed to drying winds and direct sunlight and where heavy rains may splash soil over the foliage. Instead, remove them to a shaded, protected place for storage, an open barn or shed if available. Lacking a suitable building, you can store the trees in a nearby woods, preferably on a north or east slope.

After the trees are cut, carry or drag them several at a time to the nearest fire lane or access road, and pile them on a flatbed truck, trailer, or sled for hauling to the place where they are to be stored or bundled for shipping. An evergreen tree should *never* be dragged top first. Frozen trees should be handled with extreme care, or better yet, not handled at all. Frozen branches are brittle and break easily.

BUNDLING OR BALING

Trees that are to be shipped any great distance by truck or rail should be bundled. Tying trees in bundles makes them easier to handle during loading and unloading, and compacts them so that at least 25 percent more can be loaded on a truck or railroad car than would be possible if the trees were loose (*Fig. 57*). Moreover, bundling keeps

Figure 57. Bundled Christmas trees ready for shipment. (*Oregon State University, Extension Service*)

the trees moister and, so, fresher, and protects them from breakage. Trees should, for this reason, be bundled as soon as possible after cutting, preferably within forty-eight hours.

It is to your advantage to do anything you can to keep transportation costs to a minimum and to see that the trees arrive at their destination in good condition. This holds true even if the trees are contracted for and inspected at the loading point and hauling them is someone else's responsibility, because if a retailer gets stuck with a load of damaged trees, he is sure to find out where they came from and boycott that source the next year. Hence the need for bundling.

The spruces and firs are bundled according to size, several to a bundle. Balsam fir and Douglas-fir are best adapted to bundling because of their slender form and pliable branches. Growers have generally agreed upon the following numbers of these species per bundle:

Tree height (feet)	Number per bundle
Less than 4	10–12
4–6	4–5
6–7	4
7–8	3
8–10	2
More than 10	1

The spruces bundle less easily than the firs and fewer trees can be tied in one bundle. Pines, especially red, Scotch, and Austrian, because of their bushiness and stiff branches, must be tied or bundled individually. Even when bundled, these species are much bulkier than the spruces and firs. A truck that can haul as many as nine hundred balsam fir or Douglas-fir can only hold about five hundred pines.

Many different devices are used for bundling trees; some are homemade and others are manufactured by firms that specialize in producing equipment for Christmas-tree growers. The simplest method requires only two or three wooden horses. Place them parallel to each other, a couple of feet apart. Then lay the desired number of trees across the horse and tie twine around them at intervals short enough to bind down all major branches.

This method is slow and awkward, however, especially when working with pines, which are so bulky and stiff that it is difficult for one or two men to wrestle them into submission. So several different types of "balers" have been developed to make the job faster and easier. They all work on the funnel principle, whereby the trees are forced through a small hole to compress their limbs around the trunk and are then tied with twine or wrapped with plastic netting.

The simplest of these is operated by hand, one person feeding the trees into the funnel and the other tying or

Figure 58. Hand-operated tree bundler. Tree is inserted base first through larger opening and tied as it is pulled out the small opening. (*Ohio Forestry Association*)

wrapping them as they emerge from the small end (*Fig. 58*). For the large-scale grower, the process has been mechanized so that the baler itself draws the trees through the funnel and ties or wraps them in plastic netting automatically (*Fig. 59*). Such power-operated machines with adjustable funnel sizes will run into the hundreds of dollars to buy, but they can, with a three-man crew, bundle a thousand or more trees in an eight-hour day.

Finally, you load the bundled trees on trucks (usually open or stake-bodied trucks—*Fig. 60*), bid your first crop farewell, and start getting ready for next year's planting.

Figure 59. Mechanized tree baler does the job easier, faster, and better. (*University of Minnesota, Agricultural Extension Service*)

Figure 60. Bundled trees go up conveyer into waiting truck. (*U. S. Forest Service*)

17

GOING TO MARKET

Good trees will almost sell themselves. But much of your financial success will depend upon how well you have studied the markets and how well you take advantage of current and local market conditions. This chapter deals with some of the important principles and methods of marketing Christmas trees.

In general, there are three possible outlets for your trees: you can sell them to wholesalers, you can sell them to retailers, or you can retail them yourself. There are advantages and disadvantages to all three. But regardless of which outlet you use, your marketing activity should begin long before harvesting time. During the last year or two of your first rotation, you should begin to familiarize yourself with your intended market, get acquainted with the dealers, observe how the trees are displayed, and find out how they are priced. Such preliminary scouting not only gives you a pretty good idea how Christmas trees are bought and sold in your locality, but it makes it possible for you to start locating specific outlets. In making your rounds, talk briefly with retail lot operators and wholesalers at their places of business. Tell them that you will have some trees for sale next year; specify the number and kind. Spend most of your time with those who obviously are handling quality trees and making rapid sales. List the names and addresses of the better ones for reference next year. Then, by the time you are ready to harvest your first crop of trees, you should pretty well have settled how and where you are going to market them.

SELLING TO WHOLESALERS

This is the quickest and easiest way to get rid of your trees. Oftentimes you can sell all of them to one wholesaler, thus completing your annual stint as a salesman in a single transaction (*Fig. 61*). This saves not only all the time and effort of contacting and bargaining with a lot of buyers but also the anxiety over whether or not you will be able to sell them all in time. So if you do not have the time or the inclination to work hard at selling your trees, your best bet is to deal with a wholesaler. You pay for this convenience, however, because you must accept lower prices in this market. But many growers, who prefer the production end of the Christmas-tree business to the marketing end, are perfectly satisfied to get paid only for growing the trees and let someone else (the wholesaler) get paid for selling them. It is currently estimated that about half the plantation-grown trees reach the wholesale market.

SELLING TO RETAILERS

Selling trees to retail dealers is similar to selling to wholesalers except that you will probably be dealing with several different buyers instead of one. This means a lot more time and effort spent in locating a sufficient number of retailers to handle all your trees. The advantage, of course, is a higher income—a bigger paycheck—because you can charge more for your trees when you sell to the retail market. You are doing the job of a wholesaler, so you are entitled to the wholesaler's commission in addition to payment for the trees themselves.

Some retailers may offer to take your trees on consignment rather than to buy them outright. This means that you get paid only for those trees the retailer sells. In other words, you are risking the entire financial success of your enterprise upon his aggressiveness and ability as a salesman—while he takes no risk at all. Since the retailer's

Figure 61. Unloading trees at a wholesale yard. (*University of Minnesota, Agricultural Extension Service*)

success depends upon how well he advertises, displays, and prices his wares and how efficiently and courteously he deals with his customers, the risk of loss or failure rightfully belongs upon his shoulders. By relieving him of this risk you are very likely relieving him also of the incentive to do a good job of selling. So you would do well to reject any such offers.

CONTACTING THE BUYER

There are several ways to get in touch with prospective buyers. One of the best ways is to contact them directly during the previous Christmas season. Another way is to advertise in local newspapers, specifying numbers of available trees by species and sizes. Still another way to meet buyers is through your state Christmas-tree growers' association. Some growers' associations, for example, publish each fall a complete list of trees for sale and trees wanted by their members. This list reaches all the larger dealers in the state and its publication renders a valuable service to buyers and sellers alike.

Whatever means you use to locate prospective buyers, you should contact them not later than July. Invite them to visit your plantation to inspect your trees and discuss possible terms of sale. Needless to say, you can show off your trees best while they are still standing in the plantation.

MAKING THE SALE

The best way to avoid misunderstanding in selling your trees is to tag all the trees that are currently for sale. Better yet, tag them by grades, using a different color tag for each grade. If the growers in your state or locality do not have a standard set of grades that are commonly used, you can set up your own grading system with the help of some of the hints given in Chapter 15. The grades need not be complicated, nor more than three in number, but they should be easily applied and easily understood by the buyer. Then you can establish a fair stumpage (standing-tree) price for each grade, to be quoted to all customers alike.

A few inexperienced growers, in their anxiety to sell their trees, permit buyers to cut trees promiscuously anywhere in the plantation without supervision. It goes without saying that under these circumstances the buyer takes only the best trees. Such high grading leaves nothing but second- and third-grade trees for the next prospective buyer, who either demands drastically reduced prices or rejects the trees altogether. A cardinal rule, then, in selling Christmas trees, is that you (the grower) and the buyer should agree on which trees are to be included in the sale before any cutting is done. Moreover, if you do not do the actual cutting yourself, you should certainly be on the spot to supervise the job.

In addition to what you charge for the trees themselves, you must also include in the selling price a charge for any other service that you render the buyer, such as cutting the trees and, in some cases, delivering them to his lot. You will probably want to do your own cutting; most growers do. Whether or not you do your own hauling will depend somewhat upon the demands of the buyer, the equipment that you have, and your own preference. It is a basic principle of economics, however, that the nearer you can carry your product to the ultimate consumer, the more money you will make.

Another cardinal rule in the Christmas-tree business is to demand a written agreement, or contract, for every sale. Never depend upon a verbal agreement. Since sales are usually made many months before the trees are cut and delivered, it is too easy for an unscrupulous buyer to give you a verbal order for trees and then later find that he has ordered too many or that he can buy them cheaper elsewhere. Unless you have a binding contract you are likely to be left with last-minute cancellations, that is, if you hear from your "buyer" again at all.

It is good business to have blank contracts printed. They need not be complicated. Simply state the number of trees by sizes and species, the prices, the point of delivery, and the date of harvest or delivery. Space should also be provided for a clause assuring the buyer that his trees will be delivered in good condition, that he will not be required to accept trees that have become damaged or yellowed since the time the sale was made.

As a precaution against theft of Christmas trees, some states now have laws requiring any trucker who transports trees over the public highways to have a bill of sale or other statement of proof of his right to possess the trees (*Fig. 62*). It is your duty as a grower to know if such a law exists in your state and to be sure that anyone who transports your trees is properly protected.

Your objective as a beginning grower and seller of Christmas trees should be to build up a clientele of satisfied customers that will return year after year for more trees.

MICHIGAN DEPARTMENT OF AGRICULTURE
Plant Industry Division
SIXTH FLOOR, LEWIS CASS BUILDING, LANSING, MICHIGAN 48913

BILL OF SALE

KNOW ALL MEN BY THESE PRESENTS, That I, _____

of _____, Michigan, party of the first part, owner of the premises on which the following described Christmas trees, Evergreen boughs, or other wild trees, shrubs or vines or native plants (without roots attached) were grown, do hereby sell, grant and convey same to _____ of _____ party of the second part, for and in consideration of the sum of $1.00 and other good and valuable considerations, receipt of which is hereby acknowledged, and give my consent and permission to said party of the second part to enter upon the following described premises at any time prior to _____, and to cut, remove, transport or offer for sale the following:

Description of property sold: _____

Kind of trees or boughs: _____

Number of trees or boughs (written): _____

Legal description of land where grown:

Township	Section Number	Portion of Section	Townline Number	Range Number	County

This Bill of Sale is made in accordance with Act No. 182, Public Acts of Michigan, 1962, pertaining to the cutting, removal and transportation of Christmas trees and decorative materials within this State.

IN WITNESS WHEREOF, I have hereunto signed this Bill of Sale this _____ day of _____, A.D. 19 _____

Signed and Delivered

_____
(Legal Signature of Owner)

Witness _____
(Signature)   (Address)

Witness _____
(Signature)   (Address)

WARNING UNLESS THIS FORM IS PROPERLY COMPLETED IT DOES NOT CONSTITUTE A LEGAL BILL OF SALE.

TRUCKER

Figure 62. A bill of sale similar to this one is required by some states for anyone transporting Christmas trees over public highways. (State of Michigan, Department of Agriculture)

You can do this, of course, first by producing good trees, and second by practicing good business ethics. Be sure that the prices you ask will permit the buyer to net a good profit on his investment; take special care in harvesting and handling the trees so that they will not be damaged; and stick to the provisions of the contract.

One final admonition to the grower who is going to sell his trees to the wholesaler or retailer is *do not cut any trees until they have been sold*. Some growers have been known to cut their merchantable trees, truck them to town, and then try to peddle them from wholesaler to wholesaler or retailer to retailer. If you do this, you are putting yourself on the spot. More than likely the buyer already has all the trees he needs by the time you arrive. If not, you are more or less at his mercy because he knows that you *have* to sell your trees and that you would rather sell at cut-rate prices than suffer a total loss. A cut tree that may be worth several dollars the day before Christmas has no value at all the day after. On the other hand, an uncut tree, one that is standing in the plantation, if it is not sold this year, will probably be worth even more next year.

RETAILING YOUR OWN TREES

If you have a knack for business and for selling, and if you would like to make the most money possible from your Christmas trees, the idea of setting up your own retail lot (or lots) may appeal to you. To do this you must first familiarize yourself with the retail market in your locality at least a year or two in advance of your first harvest. Observe what goes on at various neighborhood lots. Mingle with the customers and learn their preferences and prejudices. Notice which lots do the most business and try to find out why. Is it location, selection and quality of trees, advertising, or what? When you have satisfied yourself that you have learned all you can by observing other retailers, then you can start looking for your own lot to lease the next year.

Many states require all retailers to have vendors' licenses, so you had better check into this detail early.

Location of the lot is very important. It should be on a main thoroughfare, or better still, at the intersection of two, where many passers-by may view the display. Plenty of free parking space is essential because most of the customers will come by car. The lot should be large enough to display the trees effectively, in an upright position, on racks or stands. Electricity should be readily available for lighting at night because most of your sales will be made after dark.

"CHOOSE-AND-CUT"

Another selling option that has grown in popularity in the past few years is the "choose-and-cut" or "cut-your-own" method. This is a simple switch: instead of taking your trees to the customers, you bring the customers to the trees. In other words, if your plantation is within an hour's driving distance of a large town or city, you retail the trees on the stump by permitting individual buyers to select and cut their own. Born out of the burgeoning back-to-nature and do-it-yourself movements, the idea of getting out into the fresh air and countryside to find and harvest their own Christmas trees appeals to more families every year (*Fig. 63*). Many people, especially families with children, are willing to pay premium prices to do this. It is an adventure for the kids, and the parents are assured of getting a fresh tree. The grower can afford to price his trees competitively with the urban markets because he does not have to cut, bale, and truck them or lease a retail lot in the city. And, of course, he suffers no loss in cut but unsold trees.

A successful choose-and-cut operation does require careful planning and some work, however. A simple and readily understandable pricing system must be devised. Some growers prefer to avoid confusion by charging one price for all trees. Others charge according to species, height, grade, or a combination of all three. If you do charge different prices, it is essential that the buyer be able to see why. It is best for all concerned to keep the price difference to a minimum and to mark each tree, perhaps with a color-coded ribbon, before the sale begins.

Figure 63. Choosing and cutting their own Christmas trees has become an annual ritual for many families. (*Philip H. Jones*)

Another must is ample, all-weather parking space with easy access. Other nice touches include a warming house in the colder climates, with free coffee and hot chocolate, free use of cutting tools, and free twine for tying trees to cars. A traffic-control system must be laid out so that all customers who enter the plantation must exit through a single checkout point to pay for their trees and return borrowed tools. And finally, the plantation must be constantly patrolled to assist uncertain buyers, as well as to guard against pilfering and promiscuous cutting.

ADVERTISING

Wherever you retail your trees, you should do some advertising in the local newspapers and at your lot. In both places play up the fact that these are home-grown trees, produced especially for use as Christmas trees. Your main objective in advertising is to convince the users of Christmas trees that home-grown trees in general, and *your* home-grown trees in particular, are better than imported ones. You might even have some attractive leaflets printed giving the history of your trees—when and where they were planted, what kinds you have, and so on—and present each customer with one. If you plan to stay in the retail business year after year, it might be well to adopt some sort of trademark, a distinctive tag that you could attach to every tree, perhaps. Some of the state Christmas-tree growers' associations have suitable tags for sale to their members whose trees meet certain quality standards. You have worked hard to produce good trees, now here is your chance to capitalize on their quality. Give a name to your best grade of trees and see that the name is used whenever possible—"This is a John Doe Blue Ribbon Scotch Pine." If your trees live up to your advertising, in a few years you will have established a reputation and people will begin asking for "John Doe Blue Ribbon Scotch Pine" by name, the same as they do their favorite brand of soup. Your own imagination and ingenuity in advertising and displaying your trees can make a big difference in your sales. But always remember that the best advertisement is a good product.

PRICING

What about prices? How much can you charge for your trees? Unfortunately, this is another question that has no definite answer. Prices asked and paid for Christmas trees vary all over the map—both literally and figuratively. This section discusses some of the things that affect prices. Then, using these as guides, and keeping your eye on current market trends in your own locality, you should be able to establish prices that are both competitive and profitable for you.

Quality, of course, is the first consideration: the best trees bring the highest prices. So you should price your trees according to quality or grade. But no matter what system you use to grade your trees, be sure that the differences between grades are obvious to the customer. If he can see *why* one tree is priced higher than another, he will be more likely to buy the better one.

Prices also vary by species and locality. In some states or regions, for example, Scotch pine is the favorite tree and people will pay more for this species than any other. In other places Norway spruce or Douglas fir may be the preferred species and prices will vary accordingly. Naturally, the sensible grower finds out what the two or three most popular species are in his locality before he even begins to plant and concentrates his production on these species.

The third basic price-determining factor is tree height. Larger trees bring correspondingly higher prices than smaller trees. Some growers and retailers set a minimum price for their smallest trees of certain species and grade and then have a graduated scale of prices for the larger trees. Others simply charge a flat price per foot of height for their trees.

If it were possible to establish prices on the exclusive basis of these three things—quality, species, and size— much of the guesswork could be taken out of the Christmas-tree business, and a standardized system for pricing could be developed. But so much depends upon such variables as location of the retail lots and individual retailing practices that it sometimes seems as if the basic rules of pricing are totally disregarded. Prices may differ from lot to lot with no apparent reason. But do not let this situation either bewilder or discourage you, because in spite of the apparent lack of uniformity in pricing and selling methods, people do buy Christmas trees (more and more every year, in fact) and they will patronize the places where they get their money's worth. So, regardless of whether you sell your trees to the wholesaler, to the retailer, or directly to the consumer, you should not try to price your trees so as to make a killing the first year; you should try instead to build up a clientele of satisfied customers who will remember you, your product, and your prices with pleasure and will return again next year.

18

OTHER PRODUCTS OF THE PLANTATION

In spite of all your tender and skillful care, not all your trees will make the grade for the Christmas-tree market. Some of them will inevitably be stunted, poorly shaped, or even deformed as a result of insect or disease injury, mechanical damage, or adverse site or weather conditions. Whatever the cause, there are several ways to salvage all or parts of these cull trees and still make a profit from them.

BALLED TREES FOR LANDSCAPING

Many of the rejected trees left after a Christmas-tree harvest are just as healthy as those taken, and if they are moved to a new site and shaped as desired by shearing, they make excellent landscaping stock. Some buyers even prefer a crooked or lopsided tree over a symmetrical one for ornamental use. Trees intended for this market must be dug up and balled. If the buyer is willing to do this on his own, all well and good. If not, you will have to do it yourself or hire someone else to do it. The procedure is relatively simple; but it involves some hard work, especially on larger trees.

First, scrape away the surface layer of soil surrounding the trunk of the tree. Then start digging down and under the roots all around the tree, disturbing the roots and the soil around them as little as possible. When you have dug the *ball* of roots completely free, lift the tree out of the hole and place it in an upright position on a square of burlap large enough to wrap the ball. Lift each corner of the burlap in turn, pull it snugly against the ball, twist the end around the trunk of the tree, and pin it in place with nails. Needless to say, balling can best be done in heavy soils containing a lot of clay because such soil will cling to the roots, forming a ball that can be removed from the hole intact. Lighter sandy soils do not ball so readily; oftentimes dug trees have to have their roots repacked in soil before they are wrapped, a difficult and time-consuming process.

A word of caution is necessary before you attempt to take advantage of this outlet. Some states require that anyone selling plants with roots on have a nurseryman's license, giving him legal authority to market such stock and entitling him to insect and disease inspection service. Be sure to check with the proper authorities regarding the law in your state.

POTTED CHRISTMAS TREES

There is a limited but lucrative market for small, potted Christmas trees. Such trees are used in apartments and small homes where space is limited and in larger homes as table decorations. If properly cared for, these trees may be transplanted to the yard for landscaping after serving their time as Christmas trees.

Usually trees two to three feet high are potted. Spruces, firs, and redcedars are the best species for this because they are naturally more shapely at this size than pines. To dig and pot these trees in heavy soil, force a spade into the soil all around the tree about five or six inches away from the stem. Then gently pry upward with the spade until the ball of soil containing the roots can be lifted clear. With an ordinary garden trowel or similar tool, cut the ball of earth to proper size and shape and slip it into one of the containers you have provided. Various types of containers can be used—clay pots, metal cans, baskets, or special pots made from heavy roofing paper or other water-resisting paper—as long as some provision is made for drainage. Keep the soil moist at all times, but not wet. In loose, sandy soils no particular effort should be made to dig the roots in a ball. Just dig the trees up and replant them in the containers, watering freely to assure thorough moistening of all the roots.

You may want to plant a small patch of trees especially for potting. If so, it is best to prepare the soil by plowing in the fall prior to spring planting. Plant the trees about three feet apart and cultivate every year so that the lower whorl of branches can develop fully without interference from other vegetation. Usually a small area will produce all the potting trees that you can market. Let the demand control the size of your annual planting for this purpose. Here again, you must first familiarize yourself with the state laws concerning the selling and transporting of rooted plants.

BOUGHS AND GREENS

A good way to get rid of hopelessly misshapen or partially damaged trees is to cut them up and sell the branches for Christmas decorations. Thousands of tons of evergreen boughs are used annually in homes, churches, public halls, business establishments, and city streets. Although many of these greens come from small trees growing on wild land and from the tops of larger trees felled in logging, Christmas-tree growers have entered this market too.

Buyers usually require boughs to be tied in bundles, preference ranging from five to fifty pounds per bundle. Cut the branches into two-foot lengths and tie them into bundles with strong cord. Use heavy twine or light wire for the larger bundles. If you operate your own retail lot, tie the boughs into smaller bundles—one to five pounds each—and sell them in conjunction with your trees.

WREATHS AND GARLANDS

Some growers carry this business one step further and boost their profits even more by making wreaths, ropes,

Figure 64. Painted trees are popular in some sections of the country. (*Michigan State University*)

and other novelty decorations from their greens. If you have the time and patience, you can soon learn to make wreaths by hand. If you are not inclined toward handwork of this kind and you have a large supply of greens available and a good market, you might consider buying a wreath-making machine. Both hand-operated and motorized models are available for the grower who really wants to get into the business. But whatever route you take, good prices received from wholesalers, retailers, and neighborhood stores make the effort worthwhile.

PAINTED TREES

As mentioned in Chapter 16, on harvesting, in recent years, a new fashion—colored Christmas trees—has met with limited but enthusiastic acceptance in some sections of the country, especially in the larger cities. Trees are painted various colors (white, pink, blue, silver, gold, and so on) either by spraying or dipping (*Fig. 64*). As a grower you can benefit from this vogue in two ways. First, you can take advantage of the higher prices offered for such trees. Second, and more important, is that this could be an outlet for your off-color trees, trees that are healthy and have good form but have turned yellow late in the season.

Any or all of these things—balling, potting, cutting greens, and painting—can help you to use your crop more completely, and that means more profit for you. How intensively you go into such sidelines will depend upon your own inclinations as well as upon the number of leftover trees you have after harvesting. If you intend to operate your own retail lot, a good selection of these accessory products will certainly help to attract more customers than if you deal in cut trees alone.

19

PROFITS— AND TAXES

Christmas is over. Your first crop of trees has been sold and now all you have to do for a couple of months is sit back and count your money. How much money you will have to count depends upon so many different things that predictions are almost futile. And yet, as a beginning Christmas-tree grower, one of the things you are most interested in is what your net income is likely to be.

Your gross income will depend upon how many trees you have to sell, their size and quality. It is not unusual these days for a grower to get as much as three dollars each wholesale for six- to seven-foot trees of good quality. Now whenever a prospective grower hears this, his ears perk up; he gets a faraway look in his eyes, and he begins to make some mental calculations.

"Let's see now. If I plant twelve hundred trees to the acre and harvest two acres a year, that's twenty-four hundred trees or seventy-two hundred dollars. But suppose I had sixty acres and harvested ten acres a year . . . ?" With that he grabs his hat, jumps in the car, and goes out looking for land.

Regrettably, these castles in the air must soon fade. In the first place, whatever your annual income from Christmas trees finally turns out to be, it will not begin until the end of the first rotation. So, you have from five to eight years to wait before you take in any money at all. Furthermore, even though you plant twelve hundred trees to an acre, you cannot expect to harvest that many. Some will not survive the planting; others may be killed later by drought, insects, diseases, and so on. If as many as a thousand of your original twelve hundred trees are still living at the end of the rotation, you can consider your plantation successful. But not even all the trees that do survive will necessarily be salable as Christmas trees that first harvest year. Some may be too small and some may be too poorly formed. Moreover, only the best of your salable trees will bring premium prices. If you sell by grades, some of your trees will fall into the poorer grades and bring correspondingly lower prices. And if you do not sell by grades, the price you ask must be set in accordance with the average quality, not the best. So never count on selling all the trees that you plant and never count on getting top prices for all those you do sell.

COSTS

We still have not considered operating expenses. It costs money to produce Christmas trees, especially if you give them the care and protection they deserve. So, your gross income from selling your trees must be reduced by the cost of growing them before you can arrive at your net income. These costs include taxes, tools, and equipment, and the cost of the trees themselves, as well as annual operating costs. Most of the annual costs, such as for planting, mowing, shearing, and harvesting, will be more or less fixed, varying only with the size of your plantation. But the cost of protecting the plantation, especially from insects and diseases, may vary greatly from year to year, depending upon if and when your locality suffers any serious outbreaks.

Some growers have estimated that it costs them about three dollars to grow a harvestable tree. This includes the cost of planting and caring for the trees that eventually die or for some other reason are never harvested for Christmas trees, but it does not include the cost of the land. This is obviously a rough figure and will vary with species, location, cultural practices, and time, among other things. We quote it merely to help you in making your inevitable prognostications.

We have purposely emphasized the negative side so far in this discussion to keep you from anticipating greater profits than you will ultimately receive. But the things that are most likely to lower your gross income—low survival, damage by insects and diseases, and poor form—are things that you can do something about. So, in spite of the hazards inherent in the business, just how much money you do make is pretty much up to you. If you do everything you can to produce good trees at a low cost, you are almost sure to be financially successful.

TAXES

Whatever your profits turn out to be, you are going to have to share some of them with Uncle Sam, and probably with the state you live in. Computing income taxes, both federal and state, can be a difficult, sometimes frustrating, task. But there is a secret to simplifying the job: keep a complete and accurate record of all costs (including labor) and income related to your operation from the very beginning. Your bookkeeping system need not be elaborate—a simple day-by-day accounting will suffice for most small Christmas-tree farms. Just be sure you don't overlook anything. Such records will prove invaluable when tax time comes.

There are two general ways to report your income from selling Christmas trees. The simplest way, and perhaps the best for the grower with a small or modest-size operation, is to treat all income as *ordinary income*. Simply subtract from your total receipts the capitalized or accrued cost of the trees sold (if not previously deducted) plus the current year's operating expenses. The result is reported as income, the tax on which is determined by the number of your exemptions and other deductions.

The other option is to report part of your income as long-term *capital gain*. As your business enlarges, you will probably find it to your advantage to adopt this method, even though the computations are somewhat more involved, because it will result in a lower taxable income.

Briefly, this is how the capital gains system works. First you determine the fair market value of the trees you sold as of the first day of the taxable year (usually January 1). The difference between this figure and the capitalized cost of the trees cut is reported as long-term gain (or loss); only 40 percent of the gain is taken into income. In addition, you subtract from the sale price of the trees the fair market value and the costs of cutting and selling them and report the difference as ordinary income.

Your estimate of the fair market value of your trees as of January 1 must be based on the best information available and not on mere guesswork. There are several legitimate ways to do this but perhaps the most practical way is on the basis of price per foot of tree height. Just divide the average price you received per tree (on the stump) by the height of the average tree to get the price per foot. Then subtract the approximate height growth during the last growing season from the average height at the time of harvesting, and you will have the average height of the trees as of January 1. The price per foot times this height times the number of trees gives a reasonable estimate of the fair market value of the trees.

To qualify for this kind of tax treatment, certain conditions must be met:

1. The trees must be evergreen and more than six years old at the time of cutting. Age is reckoned from the time of germination; that is, 2–0 seedlings that have been in the plantation for four years are considered to be six years old.
2. The trees must be severed from the roots. Income from selling balled or potted trees cannot be reported in this way.

3. The trees must be sold for ornamental purposes.
4. You must own the trees, or the right to cut them, for at least nine months before the beginning of the taxable year.

Here is a hypothetical—and grossly simplified—example showing how the two methods of computing tax compare. Assume you sold two thousand trees for $20,000 or $10 per tree. Your records show that it cost you $3 to buy and grow each tree. Your operating expense for the year was $3,000, and you have arrived at a fair market value as of January 1 of $8.25 per tree, or a total of $16,500. Your calculations would look like this:

Ordinary Income Method

Total receipts		$20,000
Less cost of trees @ $3	$6,000	
Less current operating expense	3,000	9,000
Taxable income		$11,000

Capital Gains Method

Fair market value	$16,500
Less cost of trees @ $3	6,000
Capital gain	$10,500
Total sale price	$20,000
Less fair market value (January 1)	16,500
Gross income	$ 3,500
Less operating expense	3,000
Net profit	$ 500

Under the ordinary income method, your taxable income is $11,000, while under the capital gains method it is forty percent of the capital gain, or $4,200 plus your net profit of $500, or only $4,700, a definite tax advantage.

There may be some circumstances, such as failure to sell all the trees that were cut, under which it would be more advantageous to file under the ordinary income method.

Once you elect to use the capital gains method, however, you are obligated to continue to use it year after year unless given permission to change by the Internal Revenue Service. So before you finally decide, we recommend that you compute your taxable income by both methods, and then elect the one that results in the lower tax.

We do not expect that this brief explanation and this oversimplified example will enable you to compute your taxable income without a hitch. Regulations governing income taxes, especially the parts dealing with capital gains and losses, are too long and involved to present in detail here. Our purpose has been merely to acquaint you with the two methods open to you. For further information and details about how these methods would apply to your particular situation, we suggest that you consult a local tax expert or the Internal Revenue Service.

20

A PARTING WORD

In these few pages we have attempted to introduce you to the Christmas-tree business, its problems and peculiarities as well as its rewards. If we have done no more than help you decide whether to try it for yourself, we have done well. And if you *have* decided to start your own plantation, the previous nineteen chapters should help you get off to a good start. But when you get right down to working on your own land in your particular locality, you will inevitably run into some problems that have not been answered here. For, although we have tried to squeeze as much basic information as possible between these covers, every grower encounters situations that are unique to his specific environment and must be answered on the ground. Fortunately, local help is available. So, before we turn you loose on your own, we would like to introduce you to some people who can help you when you get stuck.

CHRISTMAS-TREE GROWERS' ASSOCIATIONS

In many states and provinces the production of Christmas trees has become so extensive that the growers have found it advantageous to band themselves together in associations. The purposes of these organizations are to help develop and stabilize the industry and to facilitate the exchange of ideas and information. At their regular meetings, members consider topics of common interest, such as grading, marketing, legislation, and new equipment and techniques. Experts in various fields are invited to discuss different technical and commercial aspects of the business.

If you live in or near any of the states or provinces that have associations, it would certainly be to your advantage to join. You will have the opportunity to meet other growers, many of whom will have problems similar to yours, and to visit their plantations. You will be able to keep abreast of the latest developments in all the different phases of the work. And even though you may not be able to attend all the meetings, you will receive bulletins and market reports, which in themselves are worth many times the modest annual membership fee.

At the present time, there are Christmas-tree growers' associations in more than thirty states and several provinces. The best way to find out whether your state has such an association and how to get in touch with its officers is through the National Christmas Tree Association, 611 East Wells Street, Milwaukee, Wisconsin 53202 (Tel. 414 276-6410).

In 1955, leaders in ten state associations met and established the national association. The following year this organization began publishing the *American Christmas Tree Journal,* a quarterly magazine devoted to serving the needs of people who produce and market Christmas trees. Membership in this organization is well worthwhile for any serious grower, if only to get their excellent journal. In addition to its many fine technical articles on all phases of the business, its news stories, and its advertisements for everything the grower needs, an especially valuable feature of the journal is the periodic listing of new literature in the field.

STATE EXTENSION SERVICES

Each state, in conjunction with its land-grant college and agricultural experiment station, maintains a staff of experts whose duties are to convey the latest and best information on various phases of agriculture and related fields to the people who can use it. This group is called the *Extension Service,* and is supported jointly by the states and the federal government. Of particular interest are the extension forester, who can help you with planting, management, and other problems having to do with the trees themselves; the extension entomologist, who can be of invaluable help in identifying injurious insects and recommending methods of control; and the extension plant pathologist, who can do the same for tree diseases. Some of the agricultural experiment stations, with which the State Extension Services are associated, carry on research in Christmas-tree production. If you keep in close touch with the extension personnel, you will be in on the ground floor when new developments occur.

OTHER SOURCES OF HELP

You can also call upon your local county agricultural agent or farm forester when you run into new and difficult problems. These public servants usually maintain offices in the county seat or in some other centrally located town in the district they serve. They have the advantage of being familiar with conditions in their localities and so can be especially helpful in such things as locating suitable land that can be bought or leased and advising you about any specific hazards or obstacles that you are likely to encounter. And if you ever have a technical problem that they cannot solve, they can put you in touch with someone who can.

Some people like to own Christmas-tree farms but prefer to have them operated by professionals. Others may seek paid professional help only until they are off to a good start. If you are one of these, we suggest that you contact a private consulting forester. There are many consultants throughout the country, trained and experienced in forestry, capable of assuming responsibility for all or any part of your operation. Some of them even specialize in Christmas-tree work. You can get the names and addresses of all the consulting foresters in your state or region by writing to The Society of American Foresters, 5400 Grosvenor Lane, Washington, D.C. 20014.

And finally, there is a growing literature on Christmas-tree production, chiefly in the form of locally oriented pamphlets and bulletins published by states, provinces, universities, and the U.S. Forest Service that you should be familiar with. Most of these are free for the asking and may go into greater detail on some subjects than we have been able to do here. In fact, we have drawn on many of them for source material. The list is long and continually growing, so we will not attempt to include a bibliography. There are a few basic references, however, that we think would be particularly helpful to the beginning grower, wherever his location. They are listed on the following pages.

SUGGESTED LITERATURE

GENERAL

Sander, Gary H.; Joseph Buhaly; Bernard S. Douglass; and Vernon Burlison. *Growing Christmas Trees in the Pacific Northwest*. Pacific Northwest Extension Publication 6 (revised), 1976 and 1981.

Stiell, W. M., and Charles R. Stanton. *An Introduction to Christmas Tree Growing in Canada*. Publication No. 1330, Canadian Forestry Service, Ottawa, 1974 (revised 1981).

GRADING

United States Standards for Grades of Christmas Trees. Agricultural Marketing Service, U.S. Department of Agriculture, Washington, D.C., 1979.

INSECTS AND DISEASES

Christmas Tree Pest Manual. North Central Forest Experiment Station and Northeastern Area State and Private Forestry, Forest Service, U.S. Department of Agriculture, St. Paul, Minnesota, 1983.

Peterson, Glenn W., and Richard S. Smith, Jr. *Forest Nursery Diseases in the United States*. Agriculture Handbook No. 470, Forest Service, U.S. Department of Agriculture, Washington, D.C., 1973.

Wilson, Louis F. *A Guide to Insect Injury of Conifers in the Lake States*. Agriculture Handbook No. 501, Forest Service, U.S. Department of Agriculture, Washington, D.C., 1977.

MARKETING AND TAXATION

A Guide to Federal Income Tax for Timber Owners. Agriculture Handbook No. 596, Forest Service, U.S. Department of Agriculture, Washington, D.C., 1982.

Leuschner, William A., and William A. Sellers. *The Economics of Producing and Marketing Christmas Trees*. FWS 1–75, Virginia Polytechnic Institute and State University, Division of Forestry and Wildlife Resources, 1975.

PESTICIDES

Apply Herbicides Correctly: A Guide for Commercial Applicators. U.S. Department of Agriculture and U.S. Environmental Protection Agency, Washington, D.C.

Hamel, Dennis R. *Forest Management Chemicals*. Agriculture Handbook 585, Forest Service, U.S. Department of Agriculture, Washington, D.C., 1983.

Singer, James. *Pesticide Safety: Guidelines for Personnel Protection*. Forest Pest Management Methods Application Group, Forest Service, U.S. Department of Agriculture, Davis, California, 1980.

MISCELLANEOUS

Rogers, Carl A.; Lewis P. Bissell; and Conrad C. Rupert. *Christmas Tree Wreath Maker's Manual*. Bulletin 501 (revised), Cooperative Extension Service, University of Maine, Orono, 1974.

INDEX

Index